"We all have times when we need to have words with God. Addison's book takes us through our desires for prayer, our disappointments in prayer, and the profound deeper plan of God for our prayers. This is the book you'll return to again and again."

Mark Batterson, *New York Times* bestselling author
of *The Circle Maker*, lead pastor of National
Community Church in Washington, D.C.

"I want my friends who really pray to write books on prayer. That's why I'm so glad Addison has written *Words with God*. This beautifully written book is honest, intelligent, mysterious, and hope-filled. It's the kind of book about prayer that makes you want to pray."

Annie F. Downs, *New York Times* bestselling author
of *That Sounds Fun*

"If we could only learn how to pray, we just might see mountains move. Addison Bevere's words have been a guide in my pursuit to pray clear, convicted, and confident prayers. If you are seeking a more intimate and powerful experience in your relationship with our heavenly Father, *Words with God* is a must-read."

Gabe Lyons, president, Q Ideas and author of *Good Faith*

"This is the needed book on prayer. If you've ever struggled with wondering why God doesn't answer your prayers, or even why you should pray at all, Addison's words will become your trusted guide."

Bianca Juarez Olthoff, Bible teacher, preacher,
author, and church planter

"Understanding prayer is at the heart of the Christian life. Many feel confused and uncertain about how to truly connect with God through prayer. Addison takes us beyond clichés and into

the heart of God in a way that is biblical, personal, and deeply satisfying. This will stir fresh hunger for intimate conversations with God."

Jon Tyson, author of *Beautiful Resistance*, pastor of Church of the City New York, www.church.nyc

"Many Christians want to be close to God but struggle to pray consistently. In his new book *Words with God*, Addison Bevere gives readers powerful and scripturally grounded encouragement that will build their faith and teach them how to pray with sincere passion, purpose, and power. With wisdom beyond his years, Addison takes readers on an honest, intimate journey through God's Word that will help them know God more intimately."

Craig Groeschel, pastor of Life.Church and *New York Times* bestselling author of *Dangerous Prayers*

"*Words with God* frames holy conversations between the Most High and his children in some beautiful and unexpected ways. Rather than limiting them to duties to be performed or entreaties to be made, Addison challenges us to view prayer as 'an exercise of freedom. It's the only way to locate the liberty that our hearts crave.' Prayer is not something we do for God. It is something we do *with* God, an intimate union with heaven while here on earth. I found myself personally challenged to see prayer through fresh eyes. If you are ready for more, you won't be disappointed."

Lisa Bevere, *New York Times* bestselling author

"As he so often does, God placed my friend Addison Bevere's book *Words with God* in my inbox exactly when I needed it most. In a quiet and dry season in my prayer life, when God's voice feels drowned out by life's frenzied pace, Addison has equipped me to learn to hear again. My bookcase contains many treasured guides I've used to reconnect to God when prayer seems hard or ineffective, including my favorites by Philip Yancey and Richard Foster. But Addison has done more than just give us a book on prayer; he walks alongside those of us who are struggling, pastoring and mentoring us through our doubts and fears into real connection and conversation with God. I'll return to *Words with God* many times in the years to come, as it has already been so helpful to me. He asked for my endorsement as a favor to him, but Addison's book is a favor to us all."

W. Lee Warren, MD, neurosurgeon, Christian Book Award–winning author, host of *The Dr. Lee Warren Podcast*

"Addison Bevere is a trusted and faithful friend to me and the church in general, and his way with and love for the nuances of Scripture is a gift to us all. In *Words with God*, he pulls prayer from its mystical realm and moves it into the practical and experiential realm of everyday life. Prepare for your heart to be set ablaze and your mind to be captivated as you find your own words to share with God."

Brandon Cormier, lead pastor of Zeal Church

"God is the one who initiates the invitation to come near, so why is it so difficult to hear from Him? Addison has crafted a masterpiece that debunks the notion of the Father being distant and welcomes us into an engaging relationship with God. This is the sort of book that helps you connect with God and stay connected to Him. You'll be transformed."

John Bevere, author of *The Awe of God*, cofounder of Messenger International

Words
with
God

Also by Addison D. Bevere

Saints

Words
with
God

Trading Boring, Empty Prayer
for Real Connection

ADDISON D. BEVERE

Revell

a division of Baker Publishing Group
Grand Rapids, Michigan

Published by Revell
a division of Baker Publishing Group
Grand Rapids, Michigan
www.revellbooks.com

Printed in the United States of America

Library of Congress Cataloging-in-Publication Data
Names: Bevere, Addison D., 1986– author.
Title: Words with God : trading boring, empty prayer for real connection / Addison D. Bevere.
Description: Grand Rapids, Michigan : Revell, a division of Baker Publishing Group, [2023] | Includes bibliographical references.
Identifiers: LCCN 2022037643 | ISBN 9780800737016 (paperback) | ISBN 9780800742874 (casebound) | ISBN 9781493434268 (ebook)
Subjects: LCSH: Prayer—Christianity. | Prayer—Biblical teaching.
Classification: LCC BV210.3 .B486 2023 | DDC 248.3/2—dc23/eng/20221129
LC record available at https://lccn.loc.gov/2022037643

The author is represented by The FEDD Agency, Inc.

Baker Publishing Group publications use paper produced from sustainable forestry practices and post-consumer waste whenever possible.

23   24   25   26   27   28   29   7   6   5   4   3   2   1

For Sophia Grace Bevere,
The Father loves hearing your words.

Contents

Contents

PART ONE

The
Canyon

1

The Voice

When we are one with our life . . . no prayer can be denied.

George MacDonald, *What's Mine's Mine*

For God speaks again and again,
though people do not recognize it.

Job 33:14 NLT

Have you ever been alone in a great canyon? One of those caverns that traps sound waves, making them skip across surfaces and travel back to you? The reverberations are fun to manipulate, at least for a while, but eventually it gets old listening to yourself on repeat. Conversations, by definition, are supposed to involve two or more people, so it's only natural for us to want someone else to get involved.

For many of us, though, praying to God feels like yelling within a great canyon. Sometimes it may seem like someone's joining the conversation, but how can we be sure that *other* voice isn't just an echo of our own thoughts, words, desires? How can we know beyond a shadow of a doubt that we're not just having words with ourselves?

Ever since I can remember, I've wanted to hear God's voice: a loud, booming voice. Heavenly words that were clear and undeniable. Anytime I'd pray as a kid, I'd hope *that* voice would respond.

But it never did.

Another voice danced around inside of me, though.

I'd try to sort out where it came from . . . my head, my heart, my gut? If the voice came from my head, then surely it was my own thoughts, but if it came from my heart or somewhere deep in my gut, shouldn't that be God's space? We're told that Jesus lives in our hearts, so it'd make sense that that's where he speaks from . . . right?

But despite my best efforts, I had the hardest time sorting out where the voice came from.

The people who seem to know their way around prayer would tell me to pray with passion and listen more than I speak. For years, though, these instructions seemed incongruent. How can I passionately listen? If I hear something I'll pay attention to it, but if I don't, I don't. I can't listen to what's not there: either God speaks to me, or he doesn't. Just get on with telling me which one it is and how it works. This whole prayer thing feels important, so we need to get it right, right?

We often get God's words wrong, though. Even the Bible has been used to endorse behaviors and decisions that heaven knows aren't right. So how can we be sure God is talking . . . and what's the right way to talk back? Where do we go when we need to have words with God?

Scripture tells us that we knew the Voice intimately once, back in that Garden. There was no denying the voice of God; he walked with us in the cool of the day. But it would seem his voice wasn't enough. We wanted to go around the Voice, to whatever may be behind it: the knowledge of good and evil, the answers to self-sufficiency, a godlike independence. So we didn't listen to the Voice. We chose a different voice, the voice of the Accuser. This voice confirmed our suspicions. There was more to be had, and we wouldn't be happy until we had whatever "it" was. The Voice was holding out on us, keeping us from discovering our own voice.

We know how that story goes.

But what's fascinating to me is the Voice didn't stay in the Garden. It moved with us. Even after we sinned and spilled our brother's blood, the Voice showed up and kept on speaking to us. But over time fewer people heard the Voice. They were too busy building their own stuff, leveraging their newfound knowledge and skill. Largely, the Voice that unites us all was forgotten, and humankind listened to a restless voice that accused and vilified, setting the world in a violent frenzy. The Accuser had everyone's ear, and life became worse than death.

———

It's hard to hear the Voice when the Accuser is constantly speaking: Get more knowledge. Do something spectacular, for God's sake, make something of your life or throw yourself off a building. Our lives are bombarded by this voice. From the moment we're born, we're coaxed into "more." Our progress is never good enough. Our brains never smart enough. Our passion never big enough. This is the voice of our making, or I guess it would be our *un*making.

And the people around us mean well, but their words are often tainted by their own accusations: the strongholds of doubt, regret, and shame that shrink their lives into rigidity or chaos. We grow up believing that this voice is the only voice. This must be the way the universe communes with us, so we search for God within the Accuser's voice.

There are some of us who know the Accuser's voice isn't the great Voice. So we deny its supremacy and look for something else. While the Accuser is abrupt and persistent, the voice of God is subtle, wooing us into awe-filled delight. At first it sounds like a babbling brook or a tree dancing in the wind, but there's something in the sound that we didn't notice before, a resonance that quietly sings within us. Or is it actually outside of us? It's too hard to tell. In the words of the great theologian Karl Barth, "O, if we could actually hear, if we could but hear this voice that resounds so clearly within us as actually God's voice. If we could only believe. Then we could also speak."[1]

Through patience, steadfastness, and faith, some of us realize that the Voice is not just something out there; it belongs to the One in whom we live, and move, and have our being. It is within us. We've got it all backward; we're not yelling across a canyon in the dark. Our voice is an echo of the Voice. It would seem that having words with God is about joining the conversation, not starting it. The Voice is speaking.

Can you hear it?

Will you answer?

There are moments when the Voice is loud and clear. Jesus had a few of these moments—three if I'm not mistaken. But he lived in tune with the Voice, and on one of these occasions he said, "That audible voice, the One you all heard, that wasn't for me, I know the Voice. That was for you."[2] Much good it did for them. Not long after that, they wanted to kill Jesus.

I guess they didn't hear the Voice.

Jesus told us that his sheep hear his voice. He also told his disciples that he wished he could tell them things, but they wouldn't understand the words. But the Spirit would come, the One who enjoins all of creation, and help them learn the Voice. Ah, so maybe that's the Voice we can and should hear. The gentle Voice, the One whom the Father and Son are especially protective of, the One we're not supposed to grieve by confusing or denying its existence. Is this because the Voice is an intimate part of us? Are we caught up in the Voice, even when we can't hear it? Do the notes vibrate color and spill beauty into our world? Jesus did say some curious things about a marriage of dimensions; maybe we're supposed to participate in that marriage now. We listened to the wrong voice and broke the earth.[3] Do we help put things back together by listening to the still, small Voice? The One that woos and guides rather than demands and demeans?

When I think about it, the ones who seem to hear the Voice are the ones who are quiet yet articulate, tender but firm, enthused by what's to come but immersed in what's now. The kind of people who participate in a reality that is not yet real to most of us.

But we *can* experience this reality for ourselves if we relearn what it is to join the conversation, which means we must stop looking for just words and sentences and learn to pray with willing hearts and open eyes. Words are important, but there's so much more to communication. Communion is what we're truly chasing: a confluence of places, people, purposes. Paul did say that this communion is available to us all, so we mustn't settle for just communicating. Prayer—words with God—is our highest and best communion. Even when our prayers have no words.

When the prophet Isaiah heard from God, the man who just a chapter earlier had a word for everyone was at a loss for words in the presence of the One who has no beginning and no end. His response was to stop speaking: "Woe is me I must be silent."[4] And in that surrendered silence, for all of us, is the possibility to survey the interconnectedness of life. Such prayer opens us to what's ultimately real.

God is God. We are not god. And so we pray.

The world is big. We are small. And so we pray.

Evil is real. But good wins the day. And so we pray.

Jesus prayed. And so we pray.

Every day we have a choice. We can let go of our tenuous grip on reality, an act that Scripture calls "dying to self," or we can cling to a lie that *feels* less dangerous than the truth. One option comes with a vibrant prayer life that is energized by faith, hope, and love. The other option comes with fear, anxiety, and confusion because we're clinging to the illusion of control and self-sufficiency. What we don't die *to* we die *from*—that's what Jesus and Paul are getting at in Luke 9 and 1 Corinthians 15, respectively.

But even beyond Luke 9 and 1 Corinthians 15, the gospel tells us the good news that we've largely gotten God (and prayer) wrong, and that's why we should repent, stop listening to the Accuser, and return to the Voice. The Accuser has no right to dictate or deny our prayers. In fact, Scripture tells us that the Spirit and Son constantly intercede so that we, through our prayers, would know the surety and connectedness of God's presence, a surety that takes us into and through the canyon. They intercede that we may know the Voice and follow it home.[5]

And the dangerous truth is that the canyon is the pathway home. Like a child sent into the wilderness for a rite of passage, so our journey takes us into and through the silence. It's in the canyon that we wrestle with God and discover who we are and what we're capable of. It's in the canyon where empty words are exchanged for a real connection. It's in the canyon that we face off with our ideas of God, prayer, and many other things, so we can surrender to the universal mind of Christ.[6] It's in the canyon that we figure out that a "prayer life" is much more than a spiritual exercise; it's the higher consciousness that reorders and integrates life, reclaiming every bit of living (and us) as holy and necessary to God's purposes and design.

The canyon's silence helps us join our voice—our holy *amen*—with the Voice again.

For even in the canyon's echo, the Voice speaks.

2

Into Silence

Praise waits for you in silence. . . .
O you who hear prayer,
to you shall all flesh come.

Psalm 65:1–2

We do not know each other yet. We have not yet dared to be
silent together.

Maurice Maeterlinck quoted by John D. Barry, *Reactions*

I t was the first time I had ever surrendered to silence.
My life was a frenzied mess. Years had passed since I'd
last slept with any regularity; two years since I had felt any
emotional connection with God; and I was frequently using the
term *burnout* to describe my job, which just so happened to involve "doing God's work"—leading an organization that offered
translated discipleship resources to virtually every country.

But I was losing perspective. Everything about my life just felt
hard, and even easy decisions started to jeopardize my peace. I

felt ashamed of how weak and pathetic I had become. I stopped dreaming; my only focus was surviving the day.

I was unwell but had no idea what to do about it.

My wife saw what I was somehow able to hide from everyone else. I'm the kind of person who doesn't want to let anyone down. Since I'm a typical firstborn, my approach to life is shut up and do whatever it takes. If something isn't working, the "thing" isn't the problem, you are. Grow. Learn. Adapt. Try harder. Become more.

And you know what, my life, by most standards, was a success. Juli and I loved each other deeply, my kids adored me, my team and friends respected and valued me, my role as chief operating officer continued to grow in scope and opportunity, the organization I led was thriving, and I was frequently asked to consult or speak into other organizations.

I was failing successfully as my interior life disintegrated.

Most of the time, I felt as if I were working with only a fraction of myself. There were days when I would put the kids down and just sit outside their door, trying to muster the strength to walk up the stairs and out of our basement. I would do whatever I could to give my kids the best of me, which required me to get crazy good at compartmentalizing my life. I honestly believed that if I just had the right answers or training or people, I could delegate and define my world into order.

There were extended moments when compartmentalization seemed to work, but the winds of life would eventually knock down my partitions, leaving me unprotected from the storms without and within, exposing my mastery as nothing more than a farce.

The nights were the worst. I knew the sleepiness that seemed to overtake me at 10:00 p.m. was only an illusion, and that the moment I put my head on the pillow, my need for control would cause me to trade sleep for insomnia, my night hours spent in desperate attempts to bandage the fractures in my world.

After a few hours of restlessness and fruitless work, I would turn to prayer, which basically consisted of me pleading for sleep so I could function and survive whatever the next day would bring. One could say these nocturnal laments were aimed at arranging the world to my design. There were, of course, moments when I would cast my cares on God, but "casting my cares" looked a lot like me trusting God to give me what I wanted, rather than searching out what Jesus offered as an easy yoke and light burden.[1]

I'm a bit stubborn, so this breaking probably took longer than it needed to. But finally, after an especially long series of sleepless nights, I realized I couldn't do anything. Like anything . . . at all. My bodily systems were shutting down, and it scared me. As usual, I was captive to the belief that there was important work to be done, but my wife told me that the world would have to spin without my contribution. At that point, I couldn't even argue with her. After a couple hours of taking inventory of how messed up I was, I agreed to surrender, knowing that I had no idea what "surrender" even meant. I promised Juli that I would, for the first time in my life, trade activity for an extended period of stillness and solitude.

Not long after that, I said goodbye to my family and boarded a plane for a quiet spot in Florida.

There are words that form only in silence.

It was my second morning alone . . . and living in silence. The first day was basically a detox, which consisted of me feeling bad for being away from my wife, kids, and meaningful work. But after a few hours of somehow forgetting that my sanity was on the line, I came to my senses and had a breakthrough in the kitchen. Something shifted in me as an intimate and intense healing process began to do its work.

For the first time in a long time, Psalm 127 became real to me, and I went to bed in peace.

> It is in vain that you rise up early
> and go late to rest,
> eating the bread of anxious toil;
> for he gives to his beloved sleep. (v. 2)

During this season, I was taking stuff to help me sleep, sleep aids that were both natural and less than natural. When night came, my heart rate would quicken if I didn't know where my sleep aids were or if I didn't take them at the right time. Everything had to be perfect, from the time I drank my last glass of water to the minute when I turned off my phone for the night to how my pillows were arranged to how the curtains were drawn. Though based on my sleep patterns, my obsessive efforts weren't working.

With greater clarity than I'd had in a long time, I knew that God was offering a peaceful sleep that was not predicated on my ability to first work things out, or by "eating the bread of anxious toil." I was beginning to learn that peace is not found in having all the answers, it's found when we're in tune with the One who is the Answer.

So I just went to bed, like normal people do.

Early that night sleep found me, and she wrapped me in her arms until the sun chased her away. As I slowly emerged from my intoxicating sleep, an invitation traveled from my spirit to my lips. Without realizing what was happening, I heard myself say, "Prayer will become the center of your life, and I want you to write what I give you . . . will you obey me?" I had never experienced such a waking. Grasped by the moment and something *other* within me that was certainly beyond my consciousness, I whispered, "Yes."

But as my mind realized what had just happened, I started to question my response. After all, I was no expert on prayer and clearly terrible at managing what God had already given me to do. Was this just another one of my plays of productivity, a sanctified grasping of sorts?

I come from a family of writers, so I could wrap my head around the writing bit, but I felt grossly unqualified to write on *prayer*, especially considering the state of my life. After school, I did a yearlong prayer intensive with a group of eighty or so students, but that hardly qualified me for writing a book on the subject, especially considering how my anxiety, insecurity, and self-centeredness had largely squeezed the life out of my prayers.

None of this made any sense to me. A barrage of doubts took shape in my mind, and I took each of them to the Father, quite confident that either I had made the whole moment up or the message had somehow been delivered to the wrong person. But as the minutes passed, I could find no release from the reality of the morning; there was a holy residue that wouldn't wash away.

I was staying just ten minutes or so from a beach, so I wandered into the arms of nature, hoping the expanse of water and sky would open my eyes and quiet my heart. As I walked along the vacant beach, I was reminded of how Gideon, when faced with what felt like an impossible invitation, asked for multiple signs to allay his doubts. Gideon also had the gall to say, "Where the heck have you been, God? Where is the evidence of your faithfulness and deliverance? We've heard of your miracles, but all we've known is misery. Surely, you've forsaken us."[2]

Several months before this moment in Florida, we'd had a few couples over to our house for a night of prayer and worship (my wife's idea, not mine). Later that evening, once everyone's defenses were mostly down, Juli suggested that we should each share a bit on what God was doing in our lives. She went first and probably expected me to follow. I didn't. My defiant silence was palpable, and someone else graciously took my place, relieving the room of its discomfort. Eventually, everyone but me had shared. The night was getting late, and I wanted to just hide behind a prayer and send the group home. But I knew that wasn't an option. The room was waiting for me to say something, and these are the kind of people who don't let one get away with cowardly behavior.

Fine. I thought. *I'll share.*

I told the group that I felt abandoned by God's presence. That I felt used and passed over. That my spiritual life consisted of little more than empty motions. I remembered a time when I experienced the connectedness and trust that they had described as part of their own journeys with God and purpose, but my path felt like a grim march into a fog that would surely end in exhaustion and failure.

To their credit, they didn't rationalize my pain or experience. They just prayed for me. During the time of prayer, one of them shared that he believed God would redeem this pain, and there would be promise and purpose that would be born in the season of disorientation. That sounded nice, and I certainly wanted what he said to be true, but all I could do was nod and thank him. The numbness within me remained.

So there I was in Florida, carrying these moments and words with me. For the first time in years, I felt deeply connected to the Father, so somewhere in my heart, I asked for what I didn't know how to ask for. I mean, what kind of sign does one need to know that they should write a book on prayer? But the request, feeble as it was, had been made, and my heart felt lighter, almost as if the ball was back in God's court and the impossible responsibility off my shoulders.

Feeling a sense of relief, I began the walk home. As the day progressed, there were more people on the beach, and I knew I could only get away with nods as greetings for so long. Eventually someone would try to start up a conversation. This was, after all, the South, and considering my commitment to silence, that would just be awkward. I was nearly home when a kind voice with a southern drawl grabbed my attention.

"Good morning, young man."

I looked around but didn't see anyone. *Maybe, like whatever happened earlier today, I'm just imagining stuff*, I thought . . . so I just kept on walking.

"I said good morning, young man."

The voice was louder this time, and I knew it wasn't just in my head. Looking again in the direction of the voice, I could now see a kind, distinguished man on a front porch, sitting on a rocking chair. A group of trees had blocked my line of sight, but apparently he saw me. Now, this was the awkward moment that I had dreaded. A simple nod wouldn't do, especially since the gentleman already thought I had ignored him the first time. I quickly searched for the Spirit's leading, and it was clear that I was to break my silence.

"Good morning, sir," I said. "Sorry, I couldn't see you through those trees. How are you this morning?"

I expected the usual response, something along the lines of, "I'm doing well, how are you?" but this man intended to have a real conversation with me. He told me his name, Ivan, and invited me to come sit on the porch with him. I politely declined, mentioning that I needed to get back to the house before the sun took advantage of my fair complexion. He nodded and kept talking, his words forming a flood of questions that blocked my way home. Ivan wanted to know who I was, what I did, what my passions were, my favorite color, my shoe size, . . . you get the idea. An hour later, we were still talking, him sitting on the porch, me standing nearby, my feet furtively inching toward a quiet escape in the house I was staying at.

But around this time Ivan finally told me something about himself—he was battling terminal cancer, and the doctors said that he had six months.

Suddenly, getting into the house didn't seem so important. It felt providential that my silence had guided me to this moment; it was now my turn to ask the questions.

As I gently probed, Ivan shared his story with me. Although he was an unassuming man, his was the kind of life most people dream of, one full of adventure, love, and success. As a high school principal, he had transformed one of the worst schools into a Blue Ribbon school, a nearly impossible turnaround. As a chaplain and missionary, he had traveled the world, helping others and positioning them to create legacies and forge pathways of their own. And he was, even then, surrounded by two generations of family, loved and respected by his own.

But age is just a number, and Ivan was still young at heart, living with a sense that there was more for him to do. An imminent death didn't make sense to him, so Ivan's prayer was that God would give him at least ten more years. I asked him if he believed in miracles, and he said yes. We talked about the miracles we had seen and how God, in strange and beautiful ways, has a knack for making the impossible possible.

Knowing that God had invited me into a greater revelation of prayer, I offered to pray for him. By this point, he had left the porch and was now standing beside me. I laid hands on him and prayed what was in my heart. I contended for healing and wholeness with every bit of faith I could muster. If faith like a mustard seed could move mountains, then surely a molecular miracle was within the Spirit's scope of work. I had seen miracles happen, I knew that God's kingdom has a way of breaking the expected outcomes and moving into the brokenness of our lives, on every level of existence. Why shouldn't it happen in this moment?

After I prayed for Ivan, he wanted to pray for me. With tears in both of our eyes, we embraced as we offered up our amen. So be it, Father.

Three hours later, I finally made it back to the house. For me, this was the sign I needed. That morning, the Father had asked me to write on prayer, and then he led me to Ivan. Surely my new friend would be healed, and this testimony would be the anchor for what God was asking me to learn and write about.

I called my wife and told her the whole story. We decided to fast and pray for Ivan, that God would infuse him with the strength he would need to embrace the miracle. In a few days, Juli and the kids would join me in Florida for some family time, and I was thrilled that they would get to meet Ivan and his family.

The following day Ivan and I sat and talked for hours. And, yes, I actually sat on the porch this time. We talked a lot about what it means to be sons and receive from our Father in heaven. I gave him a book that I had at the house, a message on being relentless and never giving up. He read the book in less than twenty-four hours, loving every bit of it. His son-in-law, Michael, and I made plans for the families to connect once Juli and the kids arrived. We spent a day at the beach together, followed by a wonderful dinner at the place they were staying. I'll never forget just sitting outside with Michael and Ivan ... the sun had gone down, there was a slight chill in the air, but we were warmed by conversations on God's faithfulness and goodness.

The next day, their family left the house, and we parted ways, promising to stay in touch. We were all energized and encouraged by our time together, all of us hoping and praying that God would heal Ivan.

But three months later, Ivan was gone.

And none of this made any sense.

Really, God? A book on prayer?

How cruel.

We've all seen prayers go "unanswered." At least, that's the term we use when a prayer seems to have no resonance, no evidence of heaven touching earth. But for me this whole situation was more than an unanswered prayer—it felt like I had missed God, or he had betrayed me. And then there was Ivan's family ... I didn't want to tell my family what had happened to Ivan, but his family didn't have that option. Their beloved father, grandfather, husband was gone.

I know prayer is so much more than getting what we ask for, but for most of us, even if it's only on the subconscious level, prayer is judged by its effectiveness, and the measurement of effectiveness is usually based on what we can see and judge with our eyes.

And my eyes were telling me that I had missed it.

None of this seemed right.

I wanted to deny that God had led me to Ivan, but I couldn't do that, no matter how hard I tried. The Spirit of God, amid my pain, sorrow, and brokenness, continued to invite me into the mysterious truth of prayer, which looked a lot like me getting to know my doubts and being okay with them. Time passed, the seasons changed, and one day I finally offered another weak *Yes* to the Father's invitation to rediscover prayer. I largely stopped running from what God had asked me to do, knowing that, once again, I didn't know what surrender required of me.

I had heard that there was such a thing as holy doubt, but the idea of it felt messy and contradictory to me. I became more honest with my doubts, though. It was like I was giving them names and faces then placing them on a shelf so that both God and I could have a good look at them and work out what they're all about.

During this time, God showed me that even Abraham, the one whom Scripture refers to as the father of faith,[3] doubted God. His doubt led to head-scratching behavior, such as him giving his wife to other men and having sex with a servant to birth an heir. Yet Paul writes that somehow Abraham never succumbed to unbelief. That led me to search out the difference between unbelief and doubt, because surely Abraham doubted.

To put it simply, unbelief is the rejection of God himself, whereas doubt is the rejection of our *idea* of God. Unbelief is to deny God's faithfulness. Doubt is to question when or how God will be faithful. Unbelief leads to apathy. Doubt often results in premature action.

I realized that it wasn't that I doubted God's ability to do whatever he wants to do, I just doubted myself, my worthiness, perception, skill, and acumen. The truth is, God's done a lot over the years with honest doubters. Doubt, when acknowledged, spoken, and surrendered to God, transforms into faith.

To put it squarely in the form of a question: Can we even know that God is faithful until life's given us reason to doubt his faithfulness?

———

There's a striking sequence of verses in the second chapter of Paul's letter to the church at Philippi. The passage reads,

> Though he was in the form of God, [Jesus] did not count equality with God a thing to be grasped, but emptied himself, by taking the form of a servant, being born in the likeness of men. And being found in human form, he humbled himself by becoming obedient to the point of death, even death on a cross. Therefore God has highly exalted him and bestowed on him the name that is above every name, so that at the name of Jesus every knee should bow, in heaven and on earth and under the earth, and every tongue confess that Jesus Christ is Lord, to the glory of God the Father. (vv. 6–11)

In true Pauline style, we find a weaving of themes that, at first glance, don't seem to mesh; but with time and consideration, they have this way of converging and forming different dimensions of truth. These verses even contain a rhythmic structure that is more typical of a poem than Paul's usual prose, a nuance that is, unfortunately, lost in the text's translation to English. But the gist of the poem is that the hierarchy of power, including the pangs of death, was redefined by the life and sacrifice of God's beloved Son—the One whose name is above every other name—and the day will come when every knee bows to the revelation of who he is.

In most Bibles, you'll find a break between verses 11 and 12, but Paul's thought continues beyond the poem. In fact, he begins verse 12 with the Greek word *hōste* ("for this reason" or "therefore"), so he is clearly building on and continuing the thought: "Therefore, my beloved, . . . work out your own salvation with fear and trembling, for it is God who works in you, both to will and to work for his good pleasure."[4]

Let's look at the sequence of these two verses. First, Paul reminds us that we are the beloved, loved by God and safe in that love. This is the love, after all, that took on the likeness of humankind, even suffering death on a Cross, to reveal who we are and what we're called to become. This revelation of belovedness is our foundation, and it will embolden us to journey across the canyon to find the Voice. It will help us walk through the doubts that keep us from understanding God, ourselves, those around us, and what it all means. From this place of surety, we are told to do the difficult work of yielding every bit of ourselves in fear and trembling. In other words, this is hard and scary work: work that will bring us to the end of ourselves and call us beyond our small constructs, answers, and ideologies and into the *otherness* of God's ways and will. We are promised that God himself will do his work in us, and as we surrender, he will work with our will, transforming a tentative yes into a resounding "So be it!"

As I dove into the depths of prayer, this passage in Philippians became a lifeline for me. I would often pray, "Father, I don't know what to will, but I yield my will to you. As your beloved son, I trust you. Take me where I otherwise wouldn't go." We must remember that we rarely know the right answers to seek or even how to seek them, "for we do not know what to pray for as we ought."[5] But even in our silence and ignorance, God meets us with groanings that never fail to do their work.

Prayer, just as life, will always retain a form of mystery, and if anyone tells you otherwise, they're reducing God to their own image, losing sight of what prayer's purpose and design are all about. When we commune with the Eternal, there will be mystery. As Paul proclaims elsewhere, borrowing from the prophet Isaiah,

> Oh, the depth of the riches and wisdom and knowledge of God! How unsearchable are his judgments and how inscrutable his ways!
>
> "For who has known the mind of the Lord, or who has been his counselor?" (Rom. 11:33–34)

"If Paul's words are true," you may ask, "then why even bother? Why attempt participation if God is unsearchable, and his ways are impossible to understand? How are our prayers to travel the pathways of his holy understanding?" The answer is both simple and mysterious: we were made for such pathways. Just because something is mysterious does not mean that it cannot and should not be searched out. As the ones with eternity written on our hearts, we were made to understand what is now shrouded in mystery.[6] And it is only by participating, especially when we don't fully comprehend, that we begin to understand what is currently beyond us.

———

The journey of understanding prayer is circular, seasonal, cyclical. Use whatever word you like, but the end of a thing has a way of taking us back to the beginning. Once we've mastered an idea, concept, or skill, we return to what feels like a novice state because the path ahead gets longer with learning. I guess it's true that the ones who know the most claim to know the least; the wisest among us listen to learn while the immature just listen for a chance to prove what they've learned.

I often complain about what feels like a return to a previous season, fighting battles of doubt, weakness, and insecurity that I thought were long gone. But the Spirit reminds me that my journey isn't linear, traveling from point A to point B. A meaningful life is much too steep for a straight line of discovery. That's where the switchbacks come in.

If you've ever been on a switchback, you know what I mean. These paths take you back and forth, in a horizontal fashion, to help you achieve the goal of ascending and descending a steep grade. The switchbacks can feel like slow going, and if you're impatient, you can start believing that the view isn't changing, and you're not getting anywhere. But the truth is you're seeing the view from a new vantage point, and, yes, this is true for even the slowest of climbers. Your present moment is both familiar and new, and that's how it must be. It may feel like you're revisiting the pain or struggle of the past, but do not believe the lie.

Our journey through the canyon of prayer is like this. It's never static, always dynamic. That's one of the reasons why we're told to pray consistently. Things are constantly changing, and our prayers make us aware of the change, keeping us from believing the lie that we're stuck in between, just yelling into the silence.

By your patience possess your souls. (Luke 21:19 NKJV)

One of our greatest challenges to understanding and participating in prayer is that our idea of it is infected by our pursuit of the immediate. Instant results. Fast-tracked success. Microwaved food. You get the idea. So if what we want doesn't soon follow our prayers, it's tempting to just give up altogether. But as we explore and become intimate with prayer's narrative as revealed in Scripture and human history, we realize that through prayer we escape the bounds of time and join a relational frequency that envelops and energizes all of God's children, those called to be stewards of his kingdom, the Saints who see the unseen.[7]

If my use of *Saints* and *kingdom* seems strange to you, hang tight for a bit. We'll explore these ideas more later. But for now, when you see *kingdom*, think of the demonstration or evidence of God's sovereign or perfect rule; an eternal form and function that empower and sustain human and cosmic flourishing.

When we begin to view prayer as our opportunity to participate in what is ultimately true about everything, it becomes so much more than what we've primarily known it to be—that is, the mechanism to bring our requests to God. And it's only within the largeness of this vision of prayer that we can discover an integrated life of purpose that offers meaning and significance instead of a small and frustrated existence.

3

The Prayer

God gives himself to the praying ones.

E. M. Bounds, *Power Through Prayer*

I used to think the Lord's Prayer was a short prayer; but as I live longer, and see more of life, I begin to believe there is no such thing as getting through it. If a man, in praying that prayer, were to be stopped by every word until he had thoroughly prayed it, it would take him a lifetime.

Henry Ward Beecher, *Life Thoughts*

Prayer is one of those things that nearly everyone does. There is this *a priori* sense that we need to pray. Even people who do not claim a religion or would even consider themselves unspiritual are known to pray when the conditions are right or very, very wrong.

A recent survey revealed that 90 percent of Americans believe in a higher power[1]—a power that, in one way or another, is someone or something beyond us yet available to us. For many of us, prayer is an attempt to connect with that someone or something. Practices like silence, solitude, meditation, mindfulness, spoken forgiveness, and gratitude are championed by even the nonreligious as necessary for one's well-being, self-actualization, and success in today's frenzied world.

When our mental or spiritual safeguards are insufficient, we reach deeper, tapping into a vein of existence that resonates with the purity and surety of God's omnipresence. We can sense there's something *other* than what we can articulate, which leads us, often against our conscious will, into the mysterious but very real world of prayer.

It's tempting to reduce anything and everything about prayer to pithy statements and life hacks, but the pathway of real connection with God is much more exciting. Many of prayer's switchbacks cannot be understood until traveled on, and that's okay. We've been conditioned to chase convenience and ease, especially in our pursuit of God, but basic anthropology will confirm that we crave something much more adventurous. While creature comforts are nice for the skin and can surely empty our wallets, the soul instead thrives on purpose, meaningful struggle, and authentic connection.

Prayer, as God intends it, is anything but boring and predictable. It is, in a real sense, the ticket into the cosmic narrative, opening our eyes to the greater story so we can locate our scene and play our part. Will our part involve mystery? Yes. Will it include bold asking? Yes. Will it demand mountain moving? Yes. Will it require quiet trust? Yes.

Prayer is the place where all those seemingly contradictory parts of you become integrated.

Formulas are great for impersonal systems and products. But prayer is not a system, and it is anything but impersonal. There are many universal and timeless principles to prayer, and it would be foolish not to borrow from the Saints, both past and present. But a life of real connection with God will stick only if, at some point, we pay the price of making it our own. If you want a model, look to those who energize your pursuit of God, drawing you into a greater understanding of faith, hope, and love—the delightfully slippery qualities that somehow reveal eternity here and now. Listen to them and watch how they pray.

For some of us, prayer has become a mechanism to get what we want without doing the work. "Our society," writes Eugene Peterson, "is cheapened by expectations of miracles: God as a supernatural shortcut so we don't have to engage in the deeply dimensional, endlessly difficult, soaringly glorious task of being a human living by faith."[2] We'll pray for health and healing while refusing to rest, eat clean, and exercise. We'll ask for financial blessing yet reject Scripture's basic instructions on stewardship. We'll petition God for wisdom and purpose as we binge Netflix, rarely opening our lives to the Word and his ways. Now, just to be clear, I am not suggesting that our lives and pursuits must be in perfect order before we pray. Perfection, in that sense, is an illusion and the enemy of spiritual progress—or any form of progress, for that matter. Besides, God uses our prayers to perfect us, so he would never discourage us from praying, no matter how imperfect our practice may be. What I am suggesting is that we revisit *why* we pray and in doing so, gather insight into how God uses prayer to slowly, and at times suddenly, reveal his purpose, character, and power in us. Such an exploration will open our eyes to the wonder of prayer and keep us from reducing it to just another form of idolatry.

Prayer is the gateway into the miraculous, but it is also how we recognize the miraculous all around us. As Elizabeth Barrett Browning wrote,

> Earth's crammed with heaven,
> And every common bush afire with God,
> But only he who sees takes off his shoes.[3]

We live on holy ground, where every bit of matter is dancing for its Creator. The question is, Can we see our space as sacred? When we do, we realize that prayer is much more than a transaction to be performed. It is a space we inhabit, ever available to those with eyes to see, ears to hear, mouths to ask, minds to know, and hearts to feel. The holiness of prayer requires our whole lives because it is everything.

Everything that we think, feel, say, and do matters to God. His Spirit searches and uncovers the substance of our lives. And it is in and through prayer that our senses become heightened, and our thought life, so often dominated by the fear of self-preservation, finds freedom from its self-centeredness and matures into greater awareness.

As wonderful as that all sounds, it also sounds risky. How will we know success when we see it? How, still, do we know what we hear is the Voice? No matter the promise, we have a tendency toward wrestling with God for control. He shares his ways with us, and we counter with something . . . better. And by "better," I mean something that we can manage, manipulate, or control. We see this interchange played out time and time again in Scripture. One example is what happened between God and Israel at Mt. Sinai.

God had delivered his chosen people from slavery and brought them to the desert. His aim was intimacy. Through the power of covenant they were to be a nation for the nations. Holy. Beautiful. Different. A collection of royalty and priests, agents of his kingdom, in tune with the Father and his plans for our good world.[4]

But Israel rejected God's offer of relationship and countered with a religious contract. The terms:

- We'll stay at a distance.
- God can tell us what to do through a priest, but don't let him speak to us.
- We'll obey God.
- Good things will happen to us.
- Everyone's happy.

Moses's response to their terms:

Do not fear, for God has come to test you, that the fear of him may be before you, that you may not sin. (Exod. 20:20)

When we read Exodus 20:20, it sure seems like Moses is speaking out of both sides of his mouth: do not fear, God wants to see if you fear him. But Moses is, in truth, differentiating between the fear of the Lord and being scared of God. One fear is good, the other bad. The fear of the Lord is what compels us to journey into the presence of the One who is holy and other, the One who is unlike anything we've ever seen. The invitation to fear God is the call to let go of the control that comes with our small view of God and see God as he is, a terrifying invitation to be sure. But this seeing or knowing is the deepest desire of our hearts; it's what we were made for, so we mustn't shrink back. That, more or less, is what Moses is telling them (and us).

But "the people stood far off, while Moses drew near to the thick darkness where God was."[5]

One could say that Moses entered temporary darkness to find the eternal Light while Israel remained in the land of shadows. The result? Within a dozen chapters Israel is worshiping a golden calf, giving themselves over to the father of all sin—idolatry—and calling the metallic work of their hands YHWH, the name exclusively used for God. Clearly their religious contract didn't work. Their distance from God didn't save them from themselves. The law, no matter how good it was, couldn't change their hearts; only union with God could do that.[6]

As a result, instead of a nation of priests, for a time, only a single tribe, the Levites, would be people of God's presence.[7] In multiple passages, God laments Israel's deviation from his original plan for relationship.[8] Here's one of them:

> Add your burnt offerings to your sacrifices, and eat the flesh. For in the day that I brought them out of the land of Egypt, I did not speak to your fathers or command them concerning burnt offerings and sacrifices. But this command I gave them: "Obey my voice, and I will be your God, and you shall be my people. And walk in all the way that I command you, that it may be well with you." (Jer. 7:21–23)

It's easy to look at Israel and question their unbelief. These are the same people who saw the Red Sea split, a river turn to blood, and more frogs than most of us could see in a hundred lifetimes. But if we're honest, we're no different from them. We're creatures of control. And in the presence of the One who is *other*, it's easy for us to turn to forms of sophisticated idolatry, such as self-worship.

And self-worship is idolatry. It's tempting to worship self because God made us godlike. We were created to rule. We were created for glory. But we don't like the way God forges glory in us. So we look for ways to circumvent him and his plan, all so we can be captains of our fate, in control of the when, what, and how. And too many of us use prayer as a means to bypass God. (Read that sentence again.) I know I'm guilty of this. But prayer's purpose is to open our eyes to the ways of God, more specifically, the purposes of his heart. And if we do not approach prayer from a place of surrender, we will inevitably turn it into another practice of idolatry.

Jesus came onto a scene where the religious elite had lost sight of God and his plans, so they were manipulating his instructions to oppress the people and separate them from the One who is Life. They had adorned God's law with many laws of their own. It was a power play, an attempt at control. There's no question that some of these religious leaders meant well, but this elite class had created religious burdens that no one could carry, and Israel was perishing for a lack of intimacy with God.[9]

When you study Jesus's ways, you quickly see that he was reluctant to give a bunch of rules. He spoke to the heart of a matter, reminding people why rules exist. Any time the Pharisees tried to trap him with a rule (a "how"), he would frustrate their question by revealing the darkness of their hearts. The religious are generally good at "how"—the rules and such—but they normally struggle with the more important question of "Why?"

Jesus knew that if he just gave them (and us) more dos and don'ts, even if the dos and don'ts were good, the powers that be would find ways to manipulate and abuse the commands. Is it any wonder that Jesus would simply say, "Love God and love your neighbor as yourself"? It's hard to maneuver your way around that one, but you know we do try!

Religion, when left to its own devices, becomes an oppressor of the weak and marginalized. And since prayer is a "religious" practice, it easily becomes just one more thing that separates "us" from "them," feeding our self-worship.

The Pharisee, standing by himself, prayed thus: "God, I thank you that I am not like other men, extortioners, unjust, adulterers, or even like this tax collector." (Luke 18:11)

Notice the Pharisee is standing "by himself." That's his problem. His disposition toward the tax collector reflected the health of his spirituality, or lack thereof. This Pharisee was far from his broken brother, which only confirmed the broken state of his soul. The pride in his heart made this Pharisee sick and isolated, but the tax collector's prayers, offered from humility and necessity, did their healing work in his heart, reclaiming bits of him from the disintegrating power of sin.

———

How and why we pray determines how and why we live.

Prayer is so much bigger than our personal piety. It's so much more than getting what we need or want from God. It is the fountain of relationship: first with God, second with ourselves, and third with others. It is a gateway of intimacy, opening the depths and secrets of God in our fellow man. Nothing is more expansive or more powerful.

Deep down, we know this to be true. We always have.

But we cannot have a vibrant life of prayer on our own terms. There's a right way to pray, and Jesus never intended to leave us in the dark. That is why right in the middle of Jesus's longest and most comprehensive presentation on human flourishing and the way of the kingdom, he teaches us how to pray: how to have words with God. Yet Jesus didn't intend for it to be a formula that we could manipulate or repackage for our own ends.

In the Lord's Prayer, however, we do find something that looks awfully close to a formula. So when Jesus gave clear instructions on *how* to pray, people took notice. *Wait, is he giving us a formula? Something we can recite and obtain the magical powers we need to control our lives . . . and conform others to our will?*

Of course, Jesus knows that what is holy is also dangerous. Despite prayer's misuse and abuse, Jesus knew what he was doing when he taught us how to pray. We would do well to remember, though, that with the Lord's Prayer, Jesus taught us *how* to pray, not just *what* to pray. Yes, we can pray the words themselves, as I certainly do, but the words are meant to help us hear what the Voice is speaking to us today. The Prayer's sequence is also perfect, offering the pathway into living prayer. The church father Tertullian once called the Lord's Prayer a summary of the whole gospel, and I think he's right.[10]

And that is why, in this book, we will use the Lord's Prayer the way Jesus intended—not as a formula but as a path to real connection, made of words. The Lord's Prayer ("The Prayer") is The Prayer of integration, The Prayer that centers our attention on the reconciliation of all things—God and human, heaven and earth, secular and sacred, human and human, pain and promise.

I want to give you what I like to call the circle of prayer. The rest of this book will pull from these eight *p* words, but I didn't break the book into *p* sections or chapters. Life is much too integrated for that. At least it should be. Rather, I'd love for you to see prayer as the interplay of what each of these words points to. "The essence of prayer," wrote Paul Tillich, "is the act of God who is working in us and raises our whole being to Himself."[11] The prayer circle below will help us understand how God works in us, moving us beyond our small, isolated sense of self so that we can live aware of and participate in the beauty and opportunity around and within us.

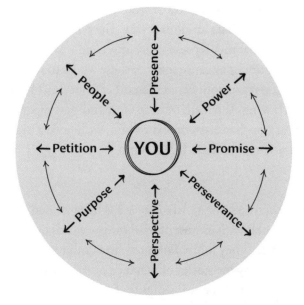

Perspective—seeing things as they truly are

Power—discovering the strength to go beyond our natural ability

Promise—finding hope when we're blinded by pain or persecution

Perseverance—contending for what is ultimately true in the face of what is partially or temporarily true

People—joining our hearts and lives with others

Petition—bringing our needs and desires to the Father

Purpose—locating our place and contribution in everyday life

Presence—knowing that the Lord is at hand and the enemy's lies overcome

Take a moment and sit with the circle. You'll probably notice that you could move the words around, placing them in different places. And that's absolutely true. The point is that all these words, and what they represent, are interconnected. Your season and disposition may cause some of these words to stand out as more necessary or connected than others, but don't be fooled: they all belong. If we are to hear God and participate in the conversations that matter most to him, we'll need a prayer life that leaves none of these facets behind.

Over the years, the Lord's Prayer has been abused and misused. So much so that most of us know the words but haven't a clue as to what they mean. For many The Prayer reeks of religiosity, tainted by memories of penance or mindless recitation. My hope is that this book will offer fresh perspective on The

Prayer that's become too familiar. The Prayer that represents the convergence of life, in every possible sense, and opens the depths of us to the movements of God's eternal Spirit.

The Lord's Prayer was a gift from the One who knows the Father best—and that is why we pray.

> Our Father in heaven,
> hallowed be your name.
> Your kingdom come,
> your will be done,
>   on earth as it is in heaven.
> Give us this day our daily bread,
> and forgive us our debts,
>   as we also have forgiven our debtors.
> And lead us not into temptation,
>   but deliver us from evil.
>
> Matt. 6:9–13

PART TWO

The
Temple

4

What We Call God

"O God" I cried and that was all. But what are the prayers of the whole universe more than expansions of that one cry? It is not what God can give us, but God that we want.

George MacDonald, *Wilfrid Cumbermede*

What comes into our minds when we think about God is the most important thing about us.

A. W. Tozer, *The Knowledge of the Holy*

Whom do you pray to? And where do you pray? When we pray, we tend to mentally go to church. Our language changes, our posture changes, and we get ready for a church mindset. That's not all bad. In the Old Testament, this was the mentality of those who approached the temple. It was the place where heaven touched earth, where people encountered a holy God, and it was a place where the out of the ordinary happened.

But when we start a prayer with this mindset, who is the God we encounter there?

Quiet your mind and identify the person or being on the other side of your prayers. Where did this image of God come from? How was it formed in your mind? Can you recall any pictures, experiences, stories, or relationships that led you to this image?

Let's go a bit deeper—how does your god respond to your pain, confusion, and brokenness? Or to your needs, desires, and longings to be loved and accepted? What causes this god to engage with your plight, to care for your requests, to heed your prayers? Does your god tolerate, like, or love you?

It's okay to stop reading this page and get alone with your thoughts. Gather some answers by sitting with these questions: *How do I see God? Why do I see God the way I do?*

You and I cannot afford to leave these questions unanswered, for how we see God determines how we see everything else. That is why one of prayer's main purposes is to help us reconcile (or integrate) our questions and pain with God's redemptive and eternal nature.

At the heart of all disintegration, both internal and external, is a wrong view of God. When something disintegrates, it breaks into particles or fragments, becoming a largely unrecognizable version of what it once was.

There is much pride in this age that refuses to embrace God in his whole (or holy) form, which means the common idea of God is easily distorted. But The Prayer challenges us to reject fragmented ideas of God, compelling us to see our Maker as both *tender Father* and *holy God*. It is when we hold on to both truths that we see God, ourselves, others, and this world as they truly are.

As you wrestle with your questions, my hope is to create an awareness that there are thoughts that need to be identified so they can be challenged, affirmed, explored, or denied. As you work through this book, I'd recommend keeping the question "How do I see God?" front and center. Your view of God is your greatest apologetic. More than anything else, it'll influence how you experience and share God in your everyday life.

———————

For years I was convinced that God was distant and angry. Sure, I heard people refer to him as "Father," but that part just didn't stick. The hellfire and brimstone sure did, though. I left many church services with the impression that God was watching me carefully, just looking for a reason to toss me into hell forever. My relationship with God was contractual, a series of dos and don'ts—when I was doing the right things, I was welcomed by him. When I messed up, I would hide from him in shame. As much as I tried to believe God was a good Father, things didn't click for me.

Many of us struggle with the idea of praying to a father because we see God through the lens of our earthly fathers. Based on what the statistics tell us, chances are you have a strained, complicated, or nonexistent relationship with your biological dad.

Maybe thoughts of your dad evoke fear and the feeling that you'll never be good enough?

Perhaps your dad was (and is) distant and emotionally unavailable to you?

Maybe you've spilled countless tears trying to work through why your father is abusive and fickle?

Or perhaps your dad just wasn't in your life, period?

"Daddy issues" has become an idiom for a Gordian knot of pain and confusion that many people spend a lifetime trying to unravel.

Considering the meanness of religiosity and the absence of fathers in homes today, you may view God as someone (or something) who is distant and impersonal. You might wonder, *Where was this heavenly Father when* [fill in the blank] *happened?* God, like your biological dad, is a presence you long to know but can never seem to corner. Someone who doesn't show up when it counts yet demands your obedience. A relational figment of your imagination, sustained by your need for protection, guidance, intimacy. You might crave paternal affection and intimacy, but your hopes have been crushed too many times, and now you are scared or unwilling to reach out to someone who just doesn't seem to be there, much less answer when you call. "The mission of the church," writes N. T. Wright, "is contained in that word [Father]; the failure of the church is highlighted by that word."[1]

Because of all the pain and disappointment known at the hands of fathers, some would argue that God is indeed the archetype of everything that's wrong with fathers: distant, judgmental, abusive, unconcerned. These enlightened minds suggest that we rise and denounce fatherly phantoms, starting with God, revealing them as the toxic perpetuators of a patriarchy that has infected our society for far too long. While it's easy and convenient to assign blame and choose scapegoats, we mustn't forget that bad fathers are still broken sons, souls caught in the fractures of sin and lost in profound pain.

When Jesus re-presented the true vision of the heavenly Father and how we should approach God in prayer, he called earthly fathers "evil,"[2] or "socially worthless, degenerate, and wicked."[3] The Greek word used here is *ponēroi* , a plural form of *ponēros*, and this word does indeed mean "evil." Jesus's use of the plural form also tells us that all earthly fathers are included in this category of evil. None are exempt. That may seem harsh, but the truth is we've all missed it with our children. Compared to my Father in heaven, my ways are evil, my decisions often transferring my own pain onto my children. That is why we fathers must lead with humility, making it clear to our children that we too are sons and rely on the heavenly Father to fill the gaps in our experience, learning, and understanding.

People tend to abandon the idea of God when they feel abandoned by him. If I were to use one word to describe what keeps us from reaching out to God, it would be our *pain*. There is a reason why much of what we know as psychotherapy involves the patient confronting his journey and relationship with pain.

Life is painful. We live in a disintegrated world, full of broken people and broken things. Sin's separating power drives us further apart, encouraging us to see everyone through a false duality of victims or villains. Most of us don't see ourselves as villains, so the Accuser uses our pain to convince us that we are lost, forgotten, and unloved by God and everyone else, for that matter. We are the victims.

The problem is, in this current age, pain is good when it is necessary. Pain locates what is wrong so it can be surrendered to what is right. When we break a bone, the pain is part of the healing process. Sure, there are ways to mitigate the pain while one heals, and a degree of relief is helpful to the process. But when we deny that something is out of joint and needing tender care, we believe a lie, setting ourselves up for only a longer and more confusing bout with pain.

If you dare, take a few minutes to gather an inventory of your most painful moments. Most likely, these memories made you bitter or better, and sometimes a bit of both. The thing about pain, though, is it never leaves us the same. It takes a lot from us, and it gives a lot to us. Suffering is what happens when our old sense of reality crashes into a new one. When life breaks us, we have a choice: will we deny the truth, deflect the truth, or dive into it?

Jesus described truth as a Rock. His message is that either we throw ourselves onto the Rock, voluntarily liberating ourselves from our small reality, or the Rock must fall on us, breaking what will never last.[4] But whatever might happen, we cannot go on living a lie, no matter how painful the truth may be. The kingdom of God must, after all, be entered through many trials and tribulations.[5]

The breaking unlocks the blessing, even when pain was the instigator.

This must be why Jesus, during the first movement of his Sermon on the Mount, pronounces blessings over groups who are wounded by the pains of a broken world. His promise to them, and to us, is that there is a greater reality, the kingdom of God, where even those of us broken by pain can find blessedness. This promise doesn't belittle the pain of the present; it does, however, offer us hope in the pain.

Jesus didn't mince words when he told us that we would have troubles in this world. But the gospel is paradoxical, so in the same breath that Jesus tells us trouble is sure to come, he also tells us that he has overcome the source of our troubles.[6] And for Jesus, the source of our troubles has a lot to do with us not *knowing* the Father, a fact that he consistently points out in John's Gospel. When we pray "Father," however, we surrender our deepest and darkest pains about fathers to what Jesus knows about the Father, a revelation he invites us to experience through prayer.

———————

Religion tries to convince us that we need access to the right person, practice, or place to get to God, thus blocking our way to the Father. But Jesus wasn't having any of that, so he tells us to "call no man your father on earth, for you have one Father, who is in heaven."[7] In other words, don't let anyone put words in the Father's mouth. Obviously, Jesus isn't telling us we can't call someone "father," but he is saying that we shouldn't allow an intermediary, whether they are a pastor, priest, or parent, to stand between us and the true nature of God. The Father wants direct and personal access to our hearts. And our search for the Father's heart is an essential part of our formation as sons and daughters and cannot be outsourced to a religious expert, no matter how holy they may appear.

Any type of formation is painful—again, that's just how this age works. The writer of Hebrews, offering us faith and hope, tells us not just to endure the process but to endure *for* the process. In other words, the process isn't just something we get through, it's the place where we find what it is to be a son or daughter. Our relationship with God isn't on the other side of the process, it's in the middle of it. By teaching us to pray "Father," Jesus is charging us to lean into the tension and surrender the effects of fatherlessness, whether they be real, perceived, or both, to the Father. This Father, unlike those who are evil, is holy Love. His name is hallowed or holy, which is a way of saying that his nature is *other* or set apart. The best of what we've seen or known in fathers are mere signposts, and not even our best scratches the surface of who God the Father is. He is holy, whole, good, perfect. He is Love. The Consuming Fire.

So many of us run from the Consuming Fire, terrified of being consumed or wounded. But the fire of God is unlike earthly fire, for the closer you get to it, the less it burns. What is real and true about you is found in the flames of Love.

In prayer, we must first do business with God's holy nature, and his knowing nature. This is what the writer of Hebrews means when we're told that God's Word is "living and active, sharper than any two-edged sword, piercing to the division of soul and of spirit, of joints and of marrow, and discerning the thoughts and intentions of the heart."[8] Such interconnectedness and knowingness can point to only the holiness of God.

These words may unnerve us, but our greatest desire is to be known and accepted, so the Father must make it clear that nothing is hidden from him. Otherwise, we could find reason to discredit his desire for us and deny his interest in our prayers. The writer of Hebrews goes on to tell us that the great High Priest, who is also our older brother—the One who reveals what relationship with the Father is all about—has made it possible for us to approach the Father with confidence, that we may receive mercy for what has been and grace for what will be.[9]

When we pray "Father," we are confronting the pain of our past by placing it in the hands of the One who promises to hold our future. In this tension of being, the pain and wounds of our past become sacred scars, reminders of how God has and will ultimately save us from all evil, drying every tear and healing every heart: "Blessed are those who mourn, for they shall be comforted."[10]

When Jesus told us to pray to the Father, he realized how difficult that would be for many of us. What is difficult, however, is often what's most meaningful, and Jesus was never one to back down from a challenge. God is Father. Period. And the Son, the One who knows the Father as he truly is, was going to do everything he could to give us a fresh vision of the Father.

Every time "Father" is whispered or shouted in prayer, we can surrender our idea of father to him. We must remember that Jesus didn't come to offer us a better religion. He came to end all religion. As the temple where heaven connects with earth, you are not embodying a new form of the old religion. You are a living testament to the relationship between God and human, heaven and earth. And that's one of the reasons why The Prayer begins with *Father*.

While in English the first word is *our*, in both Greek and Aramaic, *Father* enters the scene first, and for good reason. The revelation of Father is the foundation of prayer, a revelation perfected in and through his Son.

Jesus.

The One often mistaken as God 2.0. The One who pacifies his angry father with a brutal death and then offers us a formula prayer to get on his dad's good side, ensuring that we don't suffer a worse fate in hell. The One who jettisons the old religion to make way for a new, more robust, and, dare I say, modern religion. The One who champions grace, mercy, love and tolerates holiness, righteousness, judgment. We like Jesus, but the God of the Old Testament . . . he still gives us the creeps.

There's so much wrong with what I just wrote, but it's dangerous because I included enough distorted truth to make you pause. Yet if we're going to pray to the Father, as Jesus told us to, then we'll need to do the hard work of seeing the Father through Jesus, not seeing Jesus *instead of* the Father.

We cannot forget that Jesus emphatically says, "Whoever has

seen me has seen the Father," or that Paul writes, "For in him [Jesus] all the fullness of God was pleased to dwell."[11] There's no qualifier in either of these verses, nothing to make us believe that Jesus, in some way, is God evolved or merely the personification of God's best qualities, leaving behind anything that smells like wrath, judgment, or holiness.

Jesus came to reveal who the Father has *always* been.

Jesus is the demonstration of the Father's love, a holy Love that's been shrouded by religion but has always been there.

The true nature of the weightier matters—justice, mercy, joy, peace, faithfulness, righteousness, love, holiness—had eluded humankind, so God came in the flesh to show us what is true and eternal. With this fresh picture of God the Father, let's journey into John's Gospel.

————

John 17 is a land mine of meaningful language. Every verse brimming with blessing, offering glimpses into the mysterious and eternal intimacy between the Father and Son. An intimacy so dynamic that it stretches and reaches into the corners of the cosmos, leaving no creature behind, inviting every son and daughter to wake up, grow up, and learn Love's song.

The chapters preceding John 17, specifically chapters 14–16, create the groundswell for what I would call Jesus's most desperate and urgent attempt to reveal the Father to his brothers and sisters. Here's a sampling of statements from just John 14:

In my Father's house are many rooms. If it were not so, would I have told you that I go to prepare a place for you? (v. 2)

No one comes to the Father except through me. (v. 6)

Whoever has seen me has seen the Father. (v. 9)

I am in the Father and the Father is in me. (v. 10)

Whatever you ask in my name, this I will do, that the Father may be glorified. (v. 13)

[The Father] will give you another Helper, to be with you forever. (v. 16)

I do as the Father has commanded me, so that the world may know that I love the Father. (v. 31)

And for the record, I didn't even include all the references to the Father in John 14. (If we go back to John 5, we'll find over one hundred references to God as Father in just thirteen chapters!) As we continue into chapters 15 and 16, we're met with more facets and dimensions of God's fatherliness and what that means for us as his children. This lengthy discourse is a deluge of fatherly tenderness, full of instruction and warning, encouragement and affection, validation and promise—everything that we need to journey the treacherous and exciting road ahead.

With this context in mind, let's look at Jesus's words in chapter 17, verse 11:

Holy Father, keep them in your *name*, which you have given me, that they may be one, even as we are one. (emphasis mine)

Like with so many other verses, we can skim these words and remain unaware of the story they're telling. The story of this particular verse is about a name, a name that changes everything about how we view the Father, ourselves, and this world.

We don't often think of the power of a name. There's a chance your parents stumbled across your name while perusing a plethora of names, most likely presented in alphabetical order, which is why *A* names are among the most popular. Or maybe I just believe that because my parents gave all of us *A* names and, strangely enough, my wife and I followed the same pattern with our two sons.

But I digress. Let's get back to the power of a name.

When I say *cancer*, that name evokes something in us—maybe the memory of a loved one lost too soon. Or perhaps a season of dark nights capped by a narrow, nearly breathless escape. Growing up, for me, cancer was the name of what stole my mother's left eye.

As kids, my brothers and I would have epic dance-offs. Well, the truth is they were more like tribal rituals that would quickly transform into physical contests, often ending with tears. One of our favorite songs to get the blood pumping and testosterone spiking was the early '90s hit "Rhythm Is a Dancer" by Snap! As soon as the melodic chaos began, we were off to the races, trying to see who could forfeit their sanity first, resembling something from *Lord of the Flies*. But this song offered an unusual wrinkle that would wake us up from our frenzy, a lyric that would make us walk over to the player and turn down the volume for a few seconds: "I'm serious as *cancer* when I say rhythm is a dancer."

There was something about that line that made us cringe. There was no room for the name *cancer* in our ecstasy—it wasn't welcomed in our home.

Names are more than a collection of syllables. They reach into the essence of something to call out what is unique and specific to that person, place, or thing. God even has a history of changing names to mark new seasons or life-changing moments. In Revelation 2:17 we read that one day the conqueror will receive a new name, a name known only to the one who receives it. Clearly, names matter to God.

So what is this name that the Father gave the Son? Jesus said when we're kept in this name that we somehow share in the eternal intimacy between the Father and the Son. And not just that, there's a subtle promise that we can also know and share this divine intimacy with our brothers and sisters, here and now. But this can happen only if we are kept—"guarded" is probably a better translation—in the Father's name, which is, interestingly enough, the name of the Son as well.

So, again, what is this name?

Is it Jesus? No. (Keep in mind that "Jesus" was a popular name.)

Is it Christ(ian)? No.

Is it Saint? No.

There are two moments in Jesus's life when the Father bursts onto the scene and speaks identity over the Son. The first occurs at Jesus's baptism. As far as we know, at this point, Jesus hadn't done anything but build stuff and learn his p's and q's. There was, of course, his prodigious moment in the temple, but by most standards, Jesus's life hadn't amounted to much. He was, in a sense, a thirty-year-old who was "just getting started"—a late bloomer.

But in the third chapter of Matthew, this Son, before he did anything "worth recording" in the Gospels, was called Beloved by the Father. And on top of that, the Father expressed great pleasure in his "late bloomer." This moment was and is so significant to the gospel that it is recorded in all three of the Synoptic Gospels.

After this holy moment of divine tenderness, the Son was led into the wilderness to be tempted by the devil. For forty days and forty nights he fasted, denying himself any sustenance but the supersubstantial bread of the Father's love and pleasure—his beloved identity. When the tempter came, Jesus was hungry. For forty days his body and soul were denied food and friends. Bread never touched his lips, and a kind word didn't reach his ears. He was alone. That is, until the Accuser came.

Satan was taken aback by this enigmatic Jesus. There was something different about this God-man, and he couldn't put his finger on it. What he knew, though, is the Father had called Jesus "his beloved Son" only to then lead him to the wilderness, denying him any evidence of his fatherly affection. So what does the Accuser do? He immediately goes after Jesus's identity: "If you are the Son of God . . ."[12] In other words, prove it. Do something miraculous, spectacular, glorious. Something worthy of divine sonship.

With the limited strength left in him, Jesus responded as beloved sons and daughters must—from a place of absolute trust and confidence in the Father's love. Jesus knew who he was, so he didn't have to prove anything. He wouldn't trade his birthright for pleasure, power, or position. The devil left bewildered and defeated, yet already planning his counterattack. If he couldn't foil Jesus's mission from the top down, he would work from the bottom up, inciting the heads of religion and state to do their worst, ultimately killing the Son of Glory. Humanity's killing of God's only begotten Son would surely incite God's wrath, leading to the obliteration of the creatures that he so curiously adored. But as we know, the enemy's kill shot became God's moment of triumph—he never could understand God's plans for us because he has yet to search out

God's truest and deepest nature. He's been too busy obsessing over his own glory.

Later in Jesus's story we find another moment when the Father inserts himself into the scene. His message is too important to be left to chance, so he's less cryptic than usual. God knows our idolatrous ways and tendency toward dualistic thinking, so he gathers Moses and Elijah, symbols for the Law and the Prophets, and in their presence, the Father declares that Jesus is his beloved Son, the One whom the Law and the Prophets always pointed to. In other words, the Father wants us to know that despite the apparent tension, these three play nicely together, but listen to the Son—he will help you understand the heart and purpose of the Law and the Prophets. And then, in a dramatic fashion recorded in Matthew, Mark, and Luke, Moses and Elijah disappear, leaving Jesus alone on the mount, another sign that the Son is the Fulfillment. Everything finds its focus in him.

In both moments, the Father spoke belovedness over the Son.

God's name is Love, and the Son has always been the object of his eternal Love. He is the Beloved; that is his name. And his name, Beloved, is our place of security.

I know the word *love* has lost much of its power. We use it to describe food that we like or a series that we binge, so naturally when we hear the word, there isn't a sense of awe. In many ways, *love* has been reduced to "like" or the kind of cheap sentimentalism you find on a greeting card.

But Scripture casts love as anything but cheap and places it far beyond sentimentalism. God's love is costly Truth—the Truth Jesus gave his life to reveal. His love.

John, the beloved disciple—the one who, more than any of the apostles, understood and invited us into this revelation of

God the Father, Jesus the beloved Son, and our own beloved-ness—wrote to us,

> Beloved, let us love one another, for love is from God, and whoever loves has been born of God and knows God. Anyone who does not love does not know God, because God is love. (1 John 4:7–8)

I know these are familiar words. Words that have lost both majesty and practicality, a doubly dangerous deconstruction to be sure. But do your best to look at them with fresh eyes, see beyond the Christian truisms: even a glimpse of the Father's heart will awaken the eternity that was written on your heart. Ask yourself, what do these words mean for me? The answer is simple but not easy to grasp. It flies in the face of so much we've been programmed to believe.

The Father's name is Love, the Son's name is Beloved, and now you and I are invited to see ourselves, and our world, within this familial intimacy. We, too, are the beloved—that is our place of safety. That is our place of prayer.

Jesus prayed, ". . . that the world may know that you sent me and loved them even as you loved me. . . . I made known to them your name, and I will continue to make it known, that the love with which you have loved me may be in them, and I in them."[13] Do you see the interconnectedness? What an expansive vision of love! By revealing God's name—Love—to us, Jesus opens our lives to the world he loves.

"For God so loved the world."[14]

"By this all people will know that you are my disciples, if you have love for one another."[15]

This can happen only as we understand . . .

God is Love.

Jesus is God's beloved Son.

Jesus is God's demonstration of love for us.

We are God's beloved children.

They are God's beloved.

John goes on to tell us that the perfect love of the Father, which is the cornerstone of the reality of our belovedness, casts out or drives out fear, and this fear, which finds its footing in judgment, has no jurisdiction in the lives of the Saints, the holy sons and daughters of the Holy One, because the Father, even in judgment, executes mercy. In other words, the Father is the Consuming Fire, but his judgment is a pure expression of love. He is not the hound of heaven—he is the Father who wields a patient love that purifies and eradicates anything that does not yield to the rhythms of life.

We can love without fear when we first realize that he loves us completely and perfectly.

Jesus's name, Beloved, is above every other name. Sickness, loss, failure, and sin will never trump the power of Beloved.

> Who is to condemn? Christ Jesus is the one who died—more than that, who was raised—who is at the right hand of God, who indeed is interceding for us. Who shall separate us from the love of Christ? Shall tribulation, or distress, or persecution, or famine, or nakedness, or danger, or sword? . . .
>
> In all these things we are more than conquerors through him who loved us. For I am sure that neither death nor life, nor angels nor rulers, nor things present nor things to come, nor powers, nor height nor depth, nor anything else in all creation, will be able to separate us from the love of God in Christ Jesus our Lord. (Rom. 8:34–35, 37–39)

When we pray "Father," we are invited to lay down our definition of what it means to be "son" or "daughter" and to look to Jesus. He is the only one who truly knew the Father and what it is to be a son. He was the One who kept in perfect step with what the Father was doing, only mirroring and doing what he saw the Father doing.[16] And when he tells us to pray "Father," he is charging us to follow in his footsteps, pray like he prayed, and live like he lived. For it is only in the revelation of Father that we learn to pray (and live) like sons and daughters of God.

"To all who did receive him, who believed in *his name*, he gave the right to become children of God."[17]

5

Seeing the Kingdom

Truly, truly, I say to you, unless one is born again he cannot see the kingdom of God.

John 3:3

By virtue of . . . the incarnation, nothing here below is profane for those who know how to see.

Pierre Teilhard de Chardin, *The Divine Milieu*

The kingdom of God is often understood as something distant, abstract, or inaccessible—a heavenly reality that has little earthly relevance. Heaven, for many, is a cloudy ambiguity that somehow balances the scales of justice and helps us cope with our mortality by promising life after death. The goal, as it were, is to survive this life so we can escape to heaven one day, where every wrong will be made right, lack made whole, pain made gain. This is the hope and promise of most religions.

But when the Bible talks about the kingdom of heaven (or the kingdom of God), it has something much greater in view. As N. T. Wright puts it, "The great drama of Scripture is not fundamentally about 'how we can leave "earth" and go to live with God in "heaven,"' but *how God gets to come and live with us*."[1] This truth is what we should hold in our minds and hearts as we pray for God's kingdom to be established on earth as it is in heaven.

In the third chapter of John's Gospel, we're introduced to a Pharisee named Nicodemus, a ruler of the Jews. Jesus, at this point in John's account, hadn't done much, other than a public baptism, some disciple recruiting, a private miracle that created an abundance of wine, and a scene at the temple with a whip—a tool he fashioned himself—that was used to drive out those who had turned the temple into a place of transaction.[2]

Apparently, Jesus must have done a few other things because Nicodemus tells Jesus that "no one can do these signs [plural] that you do unless God is with him."[3]

At that time, the Jewish leaders were looking for a Davidic Messiah, a warring hero who would overcome Rome and establish God's kingdom in their midst, validating and honoring the Jewish people as God's own and judging the gentiles who had defied his holy ways and oppressed his chosen people. For them, God's kingdom wasn't just a place where they go after they die, it was a promise that God would dwell with them and displace the pagan or gentile kingdoms. The scholars knew the season had come, and there was a watchfulness among the learned. Because the time was at hand, false messiahs were popping up, but Rome made a quick end of them, revealing these "messiahs" as nothing more than impostors.

I imagine that Nicodemus had heard Jesus speak of the kingdom of God, which is what Jesus talked about more than anything else. And as a ruler of the Jews, he would have a special interest in the kingdom of God, so much so that he came to Jesus by night.

But an encounter with Jesus only made the teacher of Israel scratch his head. The kingdom, according to Jesus, would look nothing like what Nicodemus expected. Rather, Jesus spoke of a rebirth that was not of this world yet would give one eyes to see and feet to enter the hope of Israel. This process of being born again, which was a foreign idea to Nicodemus, would somehow transcend religious and ethnic tradition, creating children of the Spirit, souls enlivened by faith in the Son who reveals who the Father has always been: the hope of the nations, the reconciler of peoples, the Father of us all. In Jesus's words, "My house shall be called a house of prayer for all the nations."[4]

Fast-forward a chapter in John's Gospel, and we find Jesus in a strange place with a strange woman, a chance for us to see if what Jesus said to Nicodemus is indeed true. Could this kingdom welcome an adulterous woman who's on her way to a sixth husband? We sanitize this woman and her well, but the story is just as juicy as Jesus using jars for purification to turn water into wine. There's a reason the disciples marveled at Christ's behavior. None of this made any sense to them. They didn't have eyes to see that the fields were ripe for the harvest.

Religion, the thing that tells us when and how to pray, has a way of shrinking our lives into the scope of its control, getting us to do things on its terms and in its places. When we want forgiveness, favor, or access from God (or the gods), there are protocols to follow, people to see, places to go. That's what Nicodemus was looking for. That's what was behind the woman at the well's deflection. For them, and for us, worship is about being in the right place at the right time doing the right things. And if you take a wrong step, there's a good chance your spiritual work was for nothing. To make matters worse, the whole system is largely managed by those who represent an elite class of individuals with special access to the divine. Their religion is transactional, with clear inputs and outputs. Play by their rules, and they will grant you security and status. But if you break their rules, you could forfeit your life. At least that's what happened to Jesus.

But Jesus didn't stay dead. And his resurrection sent a clear message that what he said about temples and such was right all along.

The most sophisticated (and dangerous) forms of idolatry are the ones that use the right language, while cramming the Holy One into their religious box. These priests are no longer stewards of the mysteries of God, they are purveyors of their own "sacred" machinery, one that is bound to break the backs of its victims.[5] These teachers "shut the kingdom of heaven in people's faces" and do not enter themselves.[6] They'll even travel across sea and land to make converts that are twice as much a child of hell as they are.[7]

The true High Priest, Jesus, judged the religious world as a poor representation of the promised kingdom. Religion's strength has always lain in accusation, and the Accuser was exposed by the Light of Truth. Jesus proclaimed, "'Now is the judgment of this world; now will the ruler of this world be cast out. And I, when I am lifted up from the earth, will draw all people to myself.' He said this to show by what kind of death he was going to die."[8] Jesus spoke of the ruler of this world being cast out, even though it would seem that the true Lord of the Temple was cast out and killed by its servants.

The irony is that by casting Jesus out, these sons of Satan—Jesus's words not mine—affirmed God's intent, which has always been that holy ones make spaces sacred, and not the other way around. When Jesus breathed his last, the "curtain which made the temple a holy place, separated from other places, lost its separating power. He who was expelled as blaspheming the temple had cleft the curtain and opened the temple for everybody, for every moment."[9] "Destroy this temple, and in three days I will raise it up."[10] Jesus, in his cryptic fashion, relocated the temple, placing it within the human body. Paul would later affirm this truth, telling us that our bodies are God's temple, the dwelling place of the Spirit.[11] The temple, which always represented the place where heaven touched earth, is now us. Now we are to be that place, carriers of the sacred.

We are a dwelling place for the eternal Spirit. God's Saints made holy by his presence. Sadly, the significance of Paul's bold statement is now buried under lost context. When a first-century Christ follower heard these words, they knew the temple had represented the microcosm where heaven touched earth. Paul's words would have seemed radical, marking a "This changes everything!" moment. Prayer was no longer just a ritual or practice performed at a specific time or place. It was now an integral part of a mission that left no stone unturned. Religion, and all its practices, could no longer be compartmentalized or individualized. In a sense, religion moved out and relationship moved in. The focus shifted from buildings and practices to people and spirit. Jesus's words, "The kingdom of God is within you," were taking shape and form in their everyday lives.[12] The existing barriers between sacred and secular, Jew and Greek, slave and free, male and female, started to crumble as an ancient but forgotten vision for humanity emerged—a vision established in the person and work of Jesus, the Fulfillment of God's covenant promise to Abraham.[13] And prayer was the only way they, or we for that matter, could keep in step with the newness of the kingdom that was bursting into their lives.

The Accuser's greatest fear is that prayer would become an intimate part of us and reshape our world. He's terrified of us having words with the Father and wants to remove us from the conversation. He'd prefer the conversation be short, impersonal, and stick to religious matters. He prefers prayer to remain a slave to the Split, those past divisions of sacred and secular: a practice that is done at only the right time and in the right way.

But a sacred place is any place where God is present. A space claimed by his lordship. Our lives and everything they touch and represent are to be that space. Nothing is off-limits to his holiness, for the knowledge of the glory of God *will* cover the earth like the waters cover the seas. "There truly is," wrote Dallas Willard, "no division between sacred and secular except what we have created."[14]

Jesus also introduces a new form of priesthood. The priests before were both a barrier and a gateway. Jesus removes the barrier by laying down his life, drawing all men to himself. Meaning, we don't need to qualify who gets in and why. In fact, Jesus, when it comes to the things of God, tells us not to give others the final authority of teacher, father, or priest.[15] Our role as Saints ("holy ones" or children of the Holy One) is to bring people straight to the Father, through the work of the Son and

Spirit. Our kingdom responsibility is to be ambassadors of the good news that eternal Life is found in Jesus and that God is reconciling the world to himself, not holding its sins against it.[16] We are to proclaim that we can find freedom from sin's disintegrating power, that our lives can become whole and secure in eternal, universal love (agape). "For God did not send his Son into the world to condemn the world, but in order that the world might be saved through him."[17]

But for any of this to happen, we must first repent, which is nothing less than acknowledging that we don't see things as they really are.

———

It's humbling to admit that we don't see the world as it is.

Even what we know of the eyes' relationship with the brain encourages us to be humble in how we define reality.

The process of sight involves cones and rods in our retina that gather information about the world. The receptors pass information to our brain for processing and interpretation. What we "see" is our brain's interpretation of reality, a subjective creation and unique to our way of gathering and processing the information that is available to us.

We should also keep in mind that we selectively process what we see; otherwise, we would be overwhelmed by data and lose our ability to process what's happening around us. As we encourage selective sight, affirming its effectiveness, our process of reception becomes more focused on what has worked in the past, distorting what we see and sometimes keeping us from seeing things within our line of sight.

Have you ever noticed the phenomenon of a familiar drive that ends with a sense that you saw nothing on your way? In such cases, your brain is engaging in something called *pattern backfill*, literally using existing images of places and things rather than doing the hard work of collecting and processing new ones.

And yet we boast that our "sight" is the ultimate authority of Truth: "If I don't see it, I don't believe it." Living under that banner is a good way to see only more of what you've seen.

We don't see the world as it is. We see the world as we are.

––––––––––

When I was a freshman in high school, I learned that something was wrong with my right eye. My parents rarely had insurance while I was growing up, so we went to the doctor only when a limb was falling off. This was fine by me. I didn't mind avoiding the doctor and all the probing and pain that goes with it. But this time, the doctor came to me by way of an in-school clinic, and it wasn't long before she was staring into my eyes, for all the wrong reasons.

When the doctor scooted away from my face and gave me one of those looks, I feared the worst.

"Addison, did you know you have a cataract in your right eye?"

"A what?"

"A cataract. It's a fog on your lens that compromises your vision. You'll need to have it removed someday."

That's when she lost me. All I heard was "removed." I squirmed out of her chair and scurried back to class. Eventually, I told my parents what had happened, and they took me to an optometrist to get my eye checked out. I learned that my eye would mostly stay, which was the good news. The bad news was at some point they would need to cut out my lens and replace it with an artificial one. The doctor also told us that based on what he could tell, I likely developed the cataract from trauma in the womb or possibly a bad fall during my first year of life.

Thanks a lot, Mom.

Fifteen years later, my wife mentioned that I should see the cataract surgeon and get my eye taken care of before year's end. I knew she was right about the timing, but who voluntarily goes to get their lens cut out? Despite my better judgment, I made the appointment.

During the pre-op, the nice surgeon told me that the procedure was straightforward and the cataract, which had likely been my companion since birth, really needed to go. With the opportunity to finally see clearly staring me in the eyes, I decided to face my fears, and the surgeon exchanged the fogged lens for an artificial replacement.

Everything seemed to go as planned, but as I was preparing to leave town with my kids and wife two days later, I discovered my eye wasn't dilating, and that just didn't seem normal. Within hours of that discovery, I was lying on the same operating table, fully awake (thanks to the anesthesiologist having left for the day), doing my best to hold still while the surgeon performed an emergency procedure to stitch up my eye. Apparently, there was a snag and vitreous fluid was leaking, which could cause retinal detachment.

Our Thanksgiving plans were cancelled.

Over the next few weeks, I ended up visiting multiple eye experts and having two more procedures. It was a lot. But despite everything, when I looked through my right eye, the familiar fog still darkened and clouded my sight. The fogged lens had been replaced by a new one, but it was as if the cataract was still there. None of this made any sense. I had spent a lot of money, missed a good chunk of work, experienced the most excruciating pain of my life, and taken drugs I'd never heard of before, yet I wasn't able to see clearly.

I needed answers, so I scheduled an appointment with the cataract surgeon. After a few minutes of conversation, he looked at me and said, "Addison, your lens couldn't possibly be clearer. I can't do anything else for you. The problem is, your entire life you've seen through a fog, so your brain is still convinced that the cataract is there."

We don't see the world as it is; we see it as we are.

———

When we pray "your kingdom come, your will be done on earth as it is in heaven," we're admitting we don't see things as they are, and we're yielding to God's sight, God's understanding, God's will, and God's kingdom.

Jesus teaches us to pray like this *before* we ask for bread or try to forgive or make sense of our trials because all those things can and do take on new forms in the light of God's kingdom. The problem is, when it comes to prayer, most of us end where we should begin and begin where we should end.

When you listen to Jesus, you'll notice that he says things like, "Having eyes do you not see?"[18] In these moments, he's echoing what God has always expressed through prophets like Isaiah, Jeremiah, and Ezekiel. The prophets are known as the *seers* or "see-ers." They disrupt the common view of reality by pointing out what the rest of us miss. These seers remind us what God's kingdom is all about, especially when we become too comfortable with our own kingdoms. They call us to repent, to turn from what we've grasped as truth so we can be grasped by the Truth.

The Truth is not something that fits nicely into our small scope of vision. Jesus tells us that the eye is the lamp of the body and if the eye is bad, the whole body will be full of darkness.[19] The Accuser has a way of corrupting or darkening our view of God, ourselves, and one another, a fact we see starting in Genesis. The only way we transcend the darkness is through fixing our eyes on Jesus, who is the "light of men,"[20] and he tells us to repent, for the kingdom's sake.

Repent, for the kingdom of heaven is at hand. (Matt. 4:17)

The kingdom of God is at hand; repent and believe in the gospel. (Mark 1:15)

Repentance is what we do when we know we are blind—and wrong. Wrong about God, ourselves, and others. Repentance leads to a hope that is beyond what we've seen. A hope that connects and unites. A hope that Scripture calls the glorious inheritance in the Saints.

... having the eyes of your hearts enlightened, that you may know what is the hope to which he has called you, what are the riches of his glorious inheritance in the saints. (Eph. 1:18)

Notice the text says "in the saints." This inheritance is within us. Will we wake up and see it? Jesus said something similar when he said in Luke 17:21, "The kingdom of God is within you" (NKJV).

Many of us have been content to live in a sleepy state, seeing the world as one half awake. Well, the world needs us to wake up from our spiritual slumber. I once heard Saints described as people who wake up now instead of waiting for "then."

The writer of Hebrews collected a list of Saints, examples to inspire us on our journey. As we survey the list in Hebrews 11, its peculiarity becomes undeniable. There are kings and judges, vagabonds and outcasts, prophets and warriors—not to mention a prostitute and the son of a prostitute who have a place in the list. But what links these Saints across space and time is their ability to *see the unseen*. They participated in a reality that was not yet theirs and by doing so prophetically disrupted the status quo, setting the stage for their ultimate hope: the heavenly reality revealed in Jesus.

There was a time when the followers of Jesus were known as Saints. In the New Testament, this identifier is used more than sixty times, whereas *Christian* is used only three times. Unfortunately, when we hear the word *Saint* now, we think of stained glass windows and halos. We think of men and women who, through religious distinction, belong in a class of their own. But that is not how Scripture or the early church used the word.

Paul would often begin his letters by addressing his diverse audience as Saints. Ironically, he would do this to combat the same elitism that even today hijacks our understanding of what it is to be Saints. Keep in mind that Paul was writing to people who were just figuring out what it means to follow The Way. The ones reading his letters were Jew and gentile, slave and free, male and female. There was no distinction: no "Saints and ain'ts." Some of the Jews took issue with this because they were the holy or chosen ones, and the gentiles were unholy. But Paul knew there was no place for that kind of thinking in God's kingdom. Wherever they were from or whoever they were before didn't change the fact that they were now Saints: people of the kingdom. A fact that remains just as true for us today.

Saints is a collective identifier, not a special prefix that belongs in front of someone's name. When we look at passages like Daniel 7, we see that the Saints are the people of the kingdom. To be more accurate, they are the ones who possess the kingdom.[21] In Revelation 5, it is the prayers of the Saints that are poured out as the living creatures and elders celebrate a kingdom that will have no end.

Apparently, the prayers of the Saints matter to God . . . and to his kingdom.

These souls, raised on tiptoe, help all of us see the unseen.

6

Opening the Conversation

For we can only accept the saying "pray ceaselessly" as realistic if we say that the whole life of the saint is one mighty, integrated prayer.

Tertullian, Cyprian, and Origen, *On the Lord's Prayer*

The hour is coming when neither on this mountain nor in Jerusalem will you worship the Father. . . . The true worshipers will worship the Father in spirit and truth.

John 4:21, 23

The other day I was on the phone with a friend who's become disillusioned with God, prayer, church, and what it all means. He's a smart guy and has a way of cutting through empty sentiments with his wit and honesty.

At one point, while we were specifically talking about prayer, he said flatly, "Addison, I just don't like waking up early to have a conversation with someone who doesn't talk back. I mean, God's the only one who gets away with not showing up for a moment that he expects you to show up for daily."

My friend felt like God had let him down at a few key moments of his life, moments when he needed an answer as to where he should go and what he should do. He prayed and did what he knew to do but didn't get the answers he sought. And that just seemed like a bad deal to him.

I was glad to hear my friend's honesty. For most of his life, and likely his entire time as an adult, his faith has been little more than an intellectual exercise. He's now in a season where he needs prayer to be something more than what it's been to him, so he's headed in the right direction. I told him that God's not afraid of honesty; he just wants us to open the conversation.

We spend a lot of time with ourselves: thinking, feeling, doing. Yet for most of us, the truest parts of ourselves, known as our private world or interior life, remain largely a mystery to us and the world around us. The reason for this is simple but hard to unravel: we haven't learned how to be constant in prayer.

What if there is a way to pray without ceasing? What if we can sync our hearts with the Father's and live how the Son lived, following Jesus's example of only doing "what he sees the Father doing"? If, as the psalmist says, God cares for every detail of our lives,[1] shouldn't prayer help us see that his words are true?

We use the word *omnipresent* when describing God's presence, but I don't think we believe it. At least, we don't make it personal. Most of us, whether we admit it or not, see the world in two parts: sacred and secular. In the Christian world, "sacred" consists of the religious stuff, like church, prayer, worship. These are the places where God likes to dwell. "Secular" is a bucket for everything that isn't explicitly Christian. God doesn't really like these places. Sacred is what's eternal and important; secular is what's imminent and necessary. Prayer is too sacred for the secular parts of our lives.

Here's the problem with this view of the world, though: based on this distinction we spend most of our time in the secular world, doing secular things. We view most of our life as profane or unholy, which can cause us to believe that we're not holy. The word *profanity* comes from *pro* ("before") and *fanum* ("temple"): that is, "outside the temple." But Jesus challenges us to see ourselves as temple people and all work as sacred. No longer should we view anything or anyone as profane or unworthy of our holy attention. Duplicity and hypocrisy run wild when we believe the secular/sacred divide. We subconsciously justify behaving differently based on the place and people around us. But the kingdom of God knows no separation. Whatever we do, even the basic functions of eating and drinking, we are to be agents for the glory of God.[2]

To pray constantly is to overcome the secular/sacred divide. God is sovereign over our lives and this world. There is nothing that escapes his attention, and he invites us to see things as he sees them and reclaim every inch of his good creation.

When I first started studying what it meant to be in constant prayer, I thought the idea was ridiculous—it sounded like constant work. But eventually I realized constant prayer is a place of rest, not another form of striving. It is a rest of the heart, a holy deep breath. Such prayer keeps us reliant on God and his vision so we don't slip back into believing we are gods with our own kingdoms to build. God wants to let us in on the great secrets of life. The psalmist David wrote that God's thoughts toward us outnumber the grains of sand that are scattered across the earth.[3] One cubic foot of sand has roughly one million grains, so you do the math. That's a lot of thoughts for the Voice to share.

But most of us remain too distracted to see what's really happening around us. Our thoughts aren't fixed on higher things, so we lose hope and faith and love. Life becomes something we just get through, and the things that once brought us joy—marriage, work, kids, friends—weigh us down. We become ashamed of our decisions and attempt to keep God at arm's length, hoping to get our act together before inviting him back in. In desperation, we close the conversation, limiting our words with God to stale prayers and Sunday services.

The Father wants us to open the conversation, though. Prayer is profoundly human, touching every part of our humanity. It is only through prayer that we can know and face what we truly are and what this moment requires of us. Until we learn our lives can be a prayer, we will remain strangers to our fears and hopes, sins and desires, weaknesses and strengths. Sure, we will be aware of some of them, but we won't see them for what they truly are, nor will we have the strength and wisdom to plumb their depths.

When we surrender to prayerfulness, our hearts never stop sharing words with God. There is, after all, so much to share. Many of these words will be inarticulate and unknown to us, but they'll do their work. The Spirit and Son are constantly interceding on our behalf, quieting the murmurs and lies that keep us from yielding to the Father's will, helping us surrender every part of us to the rhythms of love.

Scripture often uses marriage metaphors to convey the connection between God and us. Let's look at the idea of constant prayer through the rhythms of a healthy marriage. The number one reason why marriages fall apart is a lack of communication. Most marriages can survive verbal spats, but when couples slide into indifference or contempt, that's a telltale sign that lawyers will soon be involved.

When it comes to communication in marriage, there are two overarching categories. Of course, there are many shades and types, but the vast majority fall within these two categories.

The first category is quality time. This is a focused time of connection, and it should not be rushed or hurried. Quality time can be spontaneous, but it is often scheduled, especially when the couple is navigating the demands and responsibilities of kids, vocation, and community. On most mornings, Juli and I spend time together before the kids are up. We sit, read our Bibles, journal, talk, and drink coffee. On Saturdays, we share an extended time together, we call it our Saturday Sits, and we also have date nights on Thursdays at least twice a month. These moments together represent our quality time.

The second category is conscious time. This is time where we are aware of each other's presence, whether we are together in person or not. One could say that this time is made possible by thoughtfulness or awareness. We are one, as the Scriptures say, and there's an interconnectedness that is inherent to marriage. To stay connected we talk, text, support, defer, serve, give, receive, listen, and so on. These actions are ongoing and spontaneous, largely a reflection of the unique challenges and opportunities of the day. Our covenant connects us, even when our days take us in different directions. Our thoughts and words reach out to each other even when we are apart.

Both conscious and quality time work together to connect us and keep us connected. In a sense, they feed off each other and are, therefore, necessary to each other.

The metaphor has its limitations, as most do, but when it comes to prayer, we need both quality time *and* conscious time with God. It is impossible to experience constancy in prayer without both. Even though Jesus lived in perfect communion with God (conscious time), he stole away for times of solitude, fasting, and prayer (quality time). Opening the conversation, therefore, doesn't mean that we abandon our prayer closet, that place of private quality time with God. It means we also let our prayer life out of the closet, into every conscious moment.

People often ask how much time they should spend alone in prayer. The answer is simple: you won't know until you try. Just make it a part of your regular routine. When I'm sharing quality time with God, sometimes I walk outside, sometimes I sit in a quiet place. Other times I'm bent over and on my knees.

As you show up consistently, your time "in the closet" will reflect what you need in your season. As with working out, the workouts themselves change as you age, but regularity is always more important than intensity. To extend the gym metaphor, if you do the same workout every time, your muscles can atrophy, so it's important to make changes *while still showing up*.

When we show up in the closet, we become more aware of how the Voice speaks outside of the closet.

———

The only way we can open the conversation and start a life of constant prayer that unites our hearts with the world is by following Jesus's example. In Jesus, we find a discipline that looks like spontaneity. He was prepared for and present in every moment and, for those reasons, knew what each moment required of him. This, of course, looked different from moment to moment and took him from place to place. If you track his movements, it will seem that Jesus almost wandered aimlessly. But as we look intently at his life and work, we find a higher form of order, call it "reorder" if you like, and he accomplished more in three years than we accomplish in a lifetime.

The secret to Jesus's success, if that's the right word for it, is his interconnectedness with the Father. As he reminds us, "I only do what I see my Father doing."[4] His life was constantly energized by this closeness with God. For him, prayer wasn't confined to a moment but stretched across moments, connecting them for an integrated purpose. His was a disciplined life, one without fracture or disintegration. The Integrator, who is the Holy Spirit, and the Son partnered together to reveal the beauty and health of union, bringing wholeness to fractured people and places.

As we'll see in a later chapter, God's intent for us is to grow up in Christ and learn The Way of the Dance. This dance is not a free-for-all, where any movements go. There are distinct steps that must be learned for the sake of everyone involved. That is what it means to follow Jesus, the One who incarnated the Dance.

During this lifetime, our bodies, which are the temple of the Spirit, are to be disciplined to follow The Way. It is with and through our bodies that we receive and share the new life of the kingdom. "Spirituality," writes Dallas Willard, "is a relationship of our embodied selves to God that has the natural and irrepressible effect of making us alive to the kingdom of God—here and now in that material world."[5]

Our spiritual growth is seen in the decisions we make with our bodies. It's with the body that we bless and curse, forgive and reconcile, protect and serve, abstain and enjoy. As Paul makes clear in his letter to the Corinthians, when we degrade our bodies (or flesh), we degrade the temple of the living God.[6] The human body is where the Good News becomes real to us and to others; therefore, it's temple property.

The apostle Paul told us to "train [*gymnazō*] yourself for godliness; for . . . godliness is of value in every way, as it holds promise for the present life and also for the life to come."[7] Peter and the writer of Hebrews also use *gymnazō* to describe our participation in God's good and formative work. This Greek word is where we get our word *gymnasium*. Life, if you will, is a gymnasium where we are formed in the ways of the kingdom. In another passage, Paul stated that he takes "pains to have a clear conscience toward both God and man."[8] The Greek word *askeō* (translated "pains") can also be translated "exercise."[9] Elsewhere we're told, also by Paul, to "work out your own salvation with fear and trembling"[10] and "cleanse ourselves from every defilement of flesh and spirit, bringing holiness to completion in the fear of God."[11]

All this talk of training, working out, and pain sounds an awful lot like hard work. And the answer is, it is! A life of godliness (the flourishing life) takes a lot of learning and unlearning. It's painful when our ideas of what is best for our lives are stripped away. We don't want to let go of our old ways and develop new habits. This is one of the reasons why Jesus told his sleepy disciples that they must "watch and pray. . . . The spirit indeed is willing, but the flesh is weak."[12]

That is also why the apostle John tells us time and again to "practice righteousness."[13] We become who we are by what we repeatedly do. The challenge is that many of us have been taught one of two common lies. The first lie is that we must earn our way to God, gathering an abundance of good works to appease his wrath and secure his good graces. This misguided belief has soured many a soul's understanding of spiritual disciplines or ascetic practices. It has certainly compromised a good number of people's understanding of prayer.

The second lie is that because of grace we don't need to do anything other than believe in Jesus's righteousness. How we live doesn't really matter because we're all just sinners saved by grace. So we should just be thankful for the Cross and do our best not to sin too badly.

Dallas Willard cut through both lies when he wrote that "grace is not opposed to effort, it is opposed to earning."[14] Our practice of righteousness helps us become who we are—Saints who can be constant in prayer. But it doesn't mean we are earning our righteousness. It does mean we make an effort.

In the book of James we're told to receive with meekness (humility) the implanted word that has the power to save our souls.[15] "Word" is *logos* in Greek. James is using *logos* in the same manner that John does: "In the beginning was the Word [*logos*], and the Word was with God, and the Word was God. . . . And the Word become flesh and dwelt among us."[16] The implanted word is what is ultimately true about God, us, and the world. It is the integration of Truth, revealed by the Spirit of Truth. Through humility, the implanted word will work its way out from the depths of us and reform every part of our lives, but this cannot happen if we don't yield to its power to save our well-being (vitality). We are, of course, saved by Jesus's life the moment of our rebirth, but our ability to experience what is already ours is determined by our ongoing yielding to what is ultimately true. Paul and Jesus call this process "dying daily." Later in the same chapter, James makes the point that we must persevere to believe what is ultimately true about ourselves; otherwise, we will live in such a way that our actions contradict our new nature. For James, how we live reflects what we believe, just as the moon reflects the sun.

So practically, what does this mean for us?

It means that we have meaningful work to do. To keep the conversation open, we must participate in the Spirit-led work that disempowers and exposes the lies around us. There are practices of mission and omission to be learned. And if we are to grow in Christ, we'll need to spend regular time in the gym of what is real so we can have the strength and perspective to know what to do and when to do it. Grace may deliver us from trying in our strength, but it requires that we train in God's strength. In Paul's words,

> I appeal to you therefore, brothers and sisters, by the mercies of God, to present your bodies as a living sacrifice, holy and acceptable to God, which is your spiritual worship. Do not be conformed to this world, but be transformed by the renewal of your mind, that by testing you may discern what is the will of God, what is good and acceptable and perfect. (Rom. 12:1–2)

The danger is that we make the disciplines an end in and of themselves. We've all known people who've forgotten the purpose of healthy eating or exercise and whose health is now compromised by the very activities that are supposed to promote their well-being. Once again, Willard has something brilliant to say on the matter:

> The activities constituting the disciplines have no value in them-
> selves. The aim and substance of spiritual life is not fasting,
> prayer, hymns, singing, frugal living, and so forth. Rather it
> is the effective and full enjoyment of active love of God and
> humankind in all the daily rounds of normal existence where
> we are placed.[17]

We open the conversation so we can know the connectedness or communion with God, ourselves, and others. This opening of self is the pathway of joy and flourishing, and it is found in the "daily rounds of normal existence."

Like with many things in life, the door in is also the door out: the entrance is also the exit. A life of awareness, which is cultivated through spiritual discipline, opens the conversation, revealing prayer's role in the connectedness of all things. But when these disciplines are misunderstood and misapplied, they will cause us to shrink back from the world God loves and seek solace in a kingdom of our own making. Prayer, for these souls, becomes a source of pride, and these souls start to sound a lot like the Pharisee who used prayer to brag about how good he was. This man may have appeared spiritually fit, but he was un-justified before God; his "goodness" fed his pride and kept him from surrendering to what is ultimately true about faithfulness, justice, and mercy.

The point of any discipline is not the action or the practice itself. We practice to play. That is why so much of practice, in any sport, prepares us to know what to do when the unexpected occurs. We must know the forms to be spontaneous, and we should know the rules before we break them. Any pursuit of artisanship or excellence requires us to believe these things. Why would it be any different for our sanctification—the journey of becoming what we already are?

The good news is we don't have to figure out the disciplines on our own. We can borrow from the ones who've practiced The Way and "loved not their lives even unto death."[18]

If you'd like to learn more about the spiritual disciplines, I suggest Dallas Willard's book *The Spirit of the Disciplines* and Richard Foster's book *Celebration of Discipline*. If you're going to choose one, go with Willard. But both books are worth the read.

Another way to open the conversation is to engage in practices that foster prayerfulness throughout the day. These practices help us become more mindful of what God is doing around and within us, helping us see how we can join and enjoy his good work. I'll highlight two practices here.

The first practice is the Ignatian Examen or the Daily Examen. It is a simple practice that takes us through a series of movements, all of which are inspired by The Prayer or other models for prayer, primarily those found in the Psalms. The steps are simple, and the idea is to take as long as you need to complete each step.

Pause and take a few deep breaths. Recognize that no matter where you are, you are in God's presence.

Bring what the psalmist calls a sacrifice of thanksgiving.[19] This is a chance for you to express gratitude for the day. Be specific and genuine. This moment of gratitude puts things into perspective.

Express your requests to the Father. This is when you are specific with your needs and desires, inviting his perspective into your struggles and opportunities.

Review the day with God. Take a journey back through the day's stirrings and struggles. Be honest about where you've ignored God's presence and guidance.

Ask for forgiveness and extend forgiveness where necessary. This is a healing step that reintegrates our heart with the Father's and our brothers and sisters.

Look forward with God and ask for his renewing power to be with you. This is where plans are made with God, where we respond and obey.

Aware of God's presence and goodness, conclude the Examen but carry with you the reality of Immanuel, "God with us."

That may seem like a lot of steps, but once you try praying the Examen, you'll notice how the steps naturally flow into each other.

Another exercise that helps open the conversation is a practice called the Daily Office. The word *office* comes from the Latin *opus* or "work." It's called the Daily Office because it is the most important work of our day, a fact that the early church championed in word and deed, and a truth that we often forget in our frenzied lives. While it was practiced by the early church, this practice predates the first century and is seen in the lives of people like Daniel and King David.

I first encountered the term *Daily Office* in Peter Scazzero's book *Emotionally Healthy Spirituality: Day by Day*. Scazzero breaks the practice into five parts: two minutes of silence and stillness, a reading of Scripture, a devotional, a question to consider, and a prayer.

The hope is that the Daily Office, like the Examen, helps create a continual awareness of God's presence; both of these practices are designed to help us grow in connectivity to God through ongoing, mutual self-revelation.

When it comes to opening the conversation, what's important is that we're consistent and present. God doesn't need you to act like the divorced parent who feels guilty for never being around and appeases the guilt by extravagant acts and promises. He just wants time with you: quality time and conscious time. Some of my favorite moments and most meaningful conversations with my wife, kids, and closest friends have happened when we weren't doing anything. We were just together.

God wants to commune with us, constantly. If it weren't true, Jesus wouldn't have told us to pray always and never give up. The challenge is, we struggle to hear the Voice when we spend most of our lives listening to the other voices. But if we continue to persevere and allow prayer to escape from its proverbial box, we will become more aware that God is never silent.

In one way or another, the Word speaks. And those who draw near hear the Voice.

As we close this chapter, I want to mention an area where we can open the conversation: our thought life. We spend a lot of time thinking. In fact, we spend more waking time processing stuff in our head than we spend forming words with our mouth.

We're learning more and more about the power of the mind and its effect on the visible world, but even thousands of years ago, Solomon wrote, "Ponder the path of your feet; then all your ways will be sure."[20] The Hebrew word translated "ponder" could also be translated "make level." In other words, right thinking leads to good living.

"The world is your kaleidoscope," wrote James Allen, "and the varying combinations of colors, which at every succeeding moment it presents to you, are the exquisitely adjusted pictures of your ever-moving thoughts."[21] We know that Mr. Allen is right, and that is why our thought life must be included in any conversation on prayer.

Scripture tells us to renew our minds so that we can be in tune with the mind of God.[22] It also tells us to take every thought captive to obey Christ.[23] Practically, we do this by surrendering our thoughts to God, in prayer. When we do, cares and worries become requests; lies bow their knee to the Truth; fears and insecurities transform into cries for help and moments of faith; thoughts of inadequacy reform into acknowledgments of dependence; feelings of joy become triggers for thanksgiving; and the list goes on.

When Paul encouraged us to pray without ceasing, I imagine he had something like what I just described in mind. It would, after all, be impossible to function while hiding in a closet or kneeling at your bed all day. This is one of the reasons why prayer, to so many, seems impractical and something that only monks or people with their backs against the wall do.

Should we have dedicated times for prayer? Absolutely. Jesus both told us to do so and modeled this way of life for us. But Jesus also lived in tune with the Father, in a way that is only possible when one's consciousness is in tune with and directed by the Spirit.

Again, that's why Jesus could say, "I only do what I see my Father doing." Some mistakenly think that such a state of consciousness would do much ill to man. "He is so heavenly minded that he is no earthly good" is not a compliment. But such split-level thinking is precisely the problem. God's aim is integration, and Spirit-led prayer is how we know that to be true.

When this age rolls up into the next, heaven and earth will be reborn as one. That is when we will know as we are known;

we will see ourselves and the world as they truly are. First Corinthians 13, the great love chapter, climaxes with this promise. And God, because he's such a good Father, wants us to know blessedness here and now. Go ahead—open the conversation and see more of God in your everyday life.

PART THREE

The
Dance

7

The Integrator

God has sent the Spirit of his Son into our hearts, crying, "Abba! Father!"

Galatians 4:6

Prayer itself is an art that only the Holy Spirit can teach us. He is the giver of all prayer.

Charles H. Spurgeon, The Power in Prayer

Have you ever thought of prayer as an art and the Spirit as your teacher?

The English poet Shelley once wrote of poetry that it "is a mirror which makes beautiful that which is distorted."[1] Prayer, too, reveals and undistorts the native beauty of God's good world, a beauty that belongs to him and the reality of his eternal kingdom.

When we engage with a great piece of art, like Rembrandt's *The Return of the Prodigal Son*, we enter a shared experience that takes on many forms. Every person's response to a work of art is unique. Even if the art is static or still, like Rembrandt's painting, it has a life to it that mirrors the life within us. We see ourselves in the painting or, at the least, we see the painting through ourselves. And this intimate interplay is what makes people fall in love with a piece of art and want to share it with others.

It's easy for us to forget that our world is God's great piece of art. The majesty of our world is a tribute to our Creator's breadth of being. "The heavens declare the glory of God," writes David, "and the sky above proclaims his handiwork. Day to day pours out speech, and night to night reveals knowledge."[2] The movements of nature compel us to search beyond our smallness, for there is beauty in the Beyond.

As humankind progresses in the sciences, we're discovering the interconnectedness of all things, a truth that art has always intuitively understood. The world is more integrated than we ever thought possible. We don't always understand the interconnectedness, but we know it's there—scientists use terms like *chaos theory* for such phenomena.

In the Genesis creation account, the Spirit of God hovers over the chaos and darkness, waiting for the proper time to form the void into a place for connection. In a similar way the Spirit hovered over the Son, marking the Son as both the guide and path back to Eden. The reality of new creation, or rebirth, would become real in him, and the Spirit, the One who is synonymous with God's creative work and power, would mark those who were reborn into this new life, granting them a new nature, one that comes with a grace to go beyond their natural ability. A grace that is accessed through the Spirit-led prayer of faith.

But here's the challenge: When faced with thousands of decisions, how are we to know which way we should go? How do we follow the One who is the Way, the Truth, and the Life when there's so much confusion and corruption in our world? How can we be people of faith in a world that leverages fear at our every turn?

———

Jesus knew that his followers would struggle to receive the truth about the kingdom, the Father, and the love that he and the Father shared. Jesus spent years living and practicing this truth before them, yet they remained myopic, the eyes of their hearts not yet enlightened by the Spirit of wisdom and revelation. So Jesus promised to send them the Helper, the Spirit of Truth, the One who knows the Father and Son better than anyone because the Spirit has always been with them, the third member of the triune dance.

> Nevertheless, I tell you the truth: it is to your advantage that I go away, for if I do not go away, the Helper will not come to you. But if I go, I will send him to you. (John 16:7)

Notice that Jesus prefaces his statement with "I tell you the truth." In other words, what I'm about to say may be difficult to believe, but I haven't lied to you before and I'm not lying to you now. For these first disciples, and for you and me as well, it's easy to believe that nothing could be better than Jesus walking with them. However, Jesus's example, while beautiful and perfect, didn't always find a home in their spirits. The example remained external, and their eyes, ears, and hearts, in so many ways, were unopened to what Jesus was doing among them.

But through the Spirit, they would begin to see through the form and into the substance. They would be able to contextualize the message because they would know the *why* behind the *what*, not losing the forest of redemption for the trees of religion. With the Spirit's help, they would be able to hear the things that Jesus wanted to tell them and learn to pray in a way that brings heaven to earth.

When it comes to prayer, it's tempting to figure out the formula, check the right boxes, and get on with our lives. But life in the Spirit can't work like that; otherwise, it would be something else entirely, and its outcome would be bondage.

Prayer is an exercise of freedom. It's the only way to locate the liberty that our hearts crave, the spaciousness of eternity. When we pray led by the Spirit, whether our prayers are grunts, groans, songs, or words unrecognizable to us, we partner with God, outside of time and space, in ways that we will fully understand when we exist outside of time. There's a peace, certainty, and freedom that comes only through submitting to the Spirit's lordship and guidance, and that includes how we pray.

The apostle Paul, the one who experienced the third heaven and things that he cannot even write about, tells us that where the Spirit is Lord over our lives, there we find freedom. He goes on to say that by contemplating the Lord's glory, or his ways, we can be transformed into his likeness by the Spirit.[3]

This is the highest form of prayer: beholding God in the Spirit. Beholding can take on many different forms, but its essence involves surrendering all our efforts to grasp God so we can be grasped by him. To behold is to *be held by*. It is to look again at the nature of God and die to our desire to be lord over any part of him.

When we pray in the Spirit, we are yielding *what we know* to what is *known by God*. We are saying yes to the One who will show us things we have never seen and take us places we could never go. Jesus explains the Spirit as a deeply formative presence that would, like the wind, blow on us from different directions, refusing to submit to our ideas of ease and effectiveness. The Spirit reminds us that we are not God and are still learning what it is to be people of The Way. And if we are to both see and enter the kingdom of God, or the reality of God with and within us, then the Spirit must take the lead.

In Hebrew, the word *ruach* is used for God's Spirit. But this word can also be used for wind or breath (vitality). Basically, the Spirit is an inescapable part of life and movement. Spirit is energy personified, but, in the same sentence, I must mention that God's Spirit cannot be confined to an impersonal something because the Spirit is Someone, possessing emotions and special protection from the Father and Son. There's a tenderness to the Spirit, an attribute that must come with searching and knowing everything about everyone, even the depths of God. To pray in or with the Spirit is to participate in a universal understanding of all things; that is how the Spirit helps us in our weakness, for we do not know how to pray. That's also why we're told to pray at all times in the Spirit.

Too often the Spirit is considered nothing more than an impersonal force or power, but that idea doesn't line up with what we see in Scripture. Jesus tabernacled with us to prove that the Spirit would soon do the same, becoming an intimate part of our internal reality. Jesus and the Spirit worked hand in hand to glorify the Father, revealing God's nature. But Jesus would leave after three years and ascend to heaven. The Spirit would remain and tabernacle or dwell among us, making our hearts home.

There's a moment in Scripture when Jesus joined his disciples for the Feast of Booths (also known as the Feast of Tabernacles) after telling them he wouldn't join them. A curious sequence, to be sure. But then again, I guess that's life with the Spirit. On the final day of the Feast of Tabernacles, a day also known as the great day, Jesus stood up and let out a cry, proclaiming himself to be the living water for all thirsty booth dwellers (sojourners).

> If anyone thirsts, let him come to me and drink. Whoever believes in me, as the Scripture has said, "Out of his heart will flow rivers of living water." (John 7:37–38)

If we stop there, it seems like Jesus is using tabernacle language to just speak of himself, but John adds a parenthetical statement to make sure we don't miss the big point . . . this is just as much about the Spirit:

> Now this he [Jesus] said about the Spirit, whom those who believed in him were to receive. (v. 39)

According to Jesus, God's Spirit nourishes our hearts with waters that flow from the presence or nature of God. These waters restore, refresh, rejuvenate, revive, release. They are the living waters of eternal life. Remember that Jesus told the Samaritan woman that this water is like a spring that wells up to eternal life. This is the life of the Spirit, the life that flows from God; it is the only water that can sustain us as we travel the pathways of new creation.

When we understand that God's intent is for each of us to become temples or tabernacles, places where the Spirit's lordship is evident in our world, we realize that prayer is where we must go to find our focus and our fuel. We are not just bystanders, slinking through life until we arrive on the other side. As beloved children, reborn of the Spirit, we are called to participate in the reality of God's kingdom, allowing God's Spirit, through prayer and surrender, to reveal the Father's heart and nature. This yielding to the Spirit is what Paul describes as the fruit or firstfruits of the Spirit.[4] Such fruit is the natural outcome of a life surrendered to the Spirit's sanctifying process, a deep work that compels us further into the holy love of Christ so we can experience freedom from sin's disintegrating power.

———————

To understand how the Spirit involves us in prayer, we need to look at the mystery of God's triune nature—the great paradox of all paradoxes. How can one be three and three be one, after all? Try explaining that to a third grader. They may never be able to do math again.

When navigating these treacherously beautiful waters, we must be cautious that in our attempts to be systematic we don't systematically dispel the majesty and otherness of God. Our Holy Father is, as Otto wrote, the *mysterium tremendum*, the Mystery that unfolds only as we acknowledge and dive into the otherness or holiness of dynamic love.[5]

In my book *Saints: Becoming More Than "Christians,"* I tackle our fear of love by tracing the word *intimacy* back to its Latin origins. *Intimacy* looks a lot like the Latin *in timor*, which means "into fear." Intimacy is the great dive into fear. And when we journey into the intimacy shared among the Triune God, we find something so *other* that the only reasonable thing for us to do is cry, with the heavenly beings, "Holy, holy, holy . . . the whole earth is full of his glory!"[6] You see, they're onto something.

They see an integrated glory that spans the globe; they know that the day will come when the knowledge of the glory of God will cover the earth like the waters cover the sea.

When we talk of God's holiness, we must remember that the greatest outworking of God's holiness is his love. More specifically, the love that is the eternal dynamism among the Father, Son, and Spirit. Their love is the womb of creation, and their unity holds everything together; their intimacy is responsible for everything that is seen and unseen. The early Saints used the Greek word *perichōrēsis* to describe this phenomenon.

Perichōrēsis is the combination of *peri* ("around") and *choreia* ("a form of dance"). Taken literally, it means to dance or flow around.

In Greek culture there is a dance that begins with at least three partners. These dancers move in perfect harmony, creating the likeness of a circle, with weaves that add motion and complexity to the movement. As the dance continues, other dancers join, finding their place in the quick but seemingly effortless dance. Eventually the dance becomes a beautiful blur, the individual dancers yielding to the greater dance, their combined individuality giving life to a collective identity.

With this in mind, let's imagine a Divine Dance.

There are three partners. The Father. The Son. And the Holy Spirit. As humans, we have a point of reference for parent/child relationships. Of course, familial relationships are often rife with dysfunction, but try to remember moments of intimacy, safety, or togetherness that pointed to something beyond human. Or if you never experienced such a moment, try to envisage what you wished or hoped for in a more innocent state, a time of faith when there was still a universe of possibilities beyond your experience or intellect. The thought or experience may be slippery, but do try to hold on to it.

"The union between the Father and Son," writes C. S. Lewis, "is such a live concrete thing that this union itself is also a Person."[7] Lewis saw the Holy Spirit as the incarnation of the love between the Father and Son. This love between the Father and Son has always existed, and because it has always existed, so has the Spirit. In other words, the Holy Spirit is the omnipresent, eternal demonstration of triune love. This Divine Love can't help but expand through creation, inviting stars and sons, creatures and comets, birds and bandits to learn the Dance. It is only in and through this love that we, those made in God's image, "live and move and have our being."[8]

While all of creation is caught up in the Dance, it is only through choice that we become active participants. Without choice the otherwise beautiful movements would become perfunctory, compromising relationship's beauty, leaving a stale taste in intimacy's mouth. God is, above all else, relational, and if we are to become mature sons and daughters of God, we must make the choice. Worship is, after all, not a matter of the right mechanics—it's an invitation to wander into the Worthy. And the One who is worthy has chosen Earth to be, as J. B. Phillips puts it, the Visited Planet.[9] The chosen context for the divine drama: the "great sculptor's shop" where one can see human statues come to life.

"It is better for you that I go away" is a promise of greater intimacy and connectedness. A promise that *what is external now will become internal then*. A promise that the Saints (then and now) could capture and share a vision of salvation and reconciliation, one that extends beyond their personal piety or security.

Just after his comment about leaving them with the Spirit as their guide, Jesus says,

> And when [the Spirit] comes, he will convict the world concerning sin and righteousness and judgment: concerning sin, because they do not believe in me; concerning righteousness, because I go to the Father, and you will see me no longer; concerning judgment, because the ruler of this world is judged. (John 16:8–11)

Evidently, we, as humanity, had failed in our understanding of and response to sin, righteousness, and judgment: the three things that Jesus calls out here. But Jesus doesn't leave us in our failures. He promises that the Holy Spirit will convict the world and illuminate the hearts of the Saints, "that they may all be one, just as you, Father, are in me, and I in you, that they also may be in us, so that the world may believe that you have sent me."[10]

The goal here, as you can see, is integration.

Sin, the first of three issues Jesus mentioned, disintegrates and kills, breaking our lives apart in every way, but God's Spirit empowers us with a grace that frees us from sin's mastery. The law, what Paul called the ministry of death,[11] could not deliver us from sin, but the Spirit transforms us by reversing and redeeming sin's fracturing power. That is why the Spirit is the Integrator, fusing us back together as we yield ourselves to kingdom reality, convicting us of what is ultimately true about God, ourselves, and others. The Spirit seals us in eternal love, empowering us to reveal the Son to the world: "By this everyone will know that you are my disciples, if you love one another."[12] Such love is possible only when we abide in Jesus through the Spirit.

Jesus also tells us that the Holy Spirit will convict the world of righteousness, the second of the three, because he goes to the Father, and we will see him no longer. Through his life and work, Jesus has reintroduced righteousness, restoring it to its familial form. Jesus specifically mentions the Father alongside righteousness to drive home the relationship between family and righteousness. Our Spirit-led lives are to reveal God's righteousness, a righteousness promised to Abraham and revealed in his Son. A righteousness that cannot be confined to written codes but is only known by being reborn in his nature: his words woven into the fabric of our new nature. A new creation work that is only possible by the Spirit.

The last thing that the world will be convicted of is judgment. According to Jesus, the ruler of this world—the Accuser—is judged. The Accuser's word about us, God, and God's world is proven false. Therefore, we should no longer trust his opinions on such matters. We don't have to believe what he says about sin and righteousness. The life, death, and resurrection of the Son have shown us what has always been true of the Father, and we can boldly declare that the Accuser has no right to judge us. The only one who can judge us is the Son, who just so happens to intercede on our behalf constantly. And because this is true, we don't have to stand in judgment over others: separating, dividing, and disintegrating. Rather, through our prayers and actions, we can be agents of forgiveness and healing. We can see sin for what it truly is and "judge" from a place of security and acceptance. Our judgments must now help others be reconciled to the Father, working with the Spirit to deliver them from the entanglements of their sins.

That is why Jesus breathed on his disciples and said, "Receive the Holy Spirit."[13] When we breathe deeply of the Spirit's power to create, heal, restore, and integrate, we can't help but breathe out a message that delivers others from the voice of the Accuser and the disintegrating effect of their sins. Jesus himself, after being led by the Spirit into the wilderness, returned in the power of the Spirit to declare the good news of the kingdom. His entire life told the story, and his prayer and connection with the Father were the strength of his service. If we are to be kingdom people, souls in tune with what God is saying to us and the world, we must be people who live in step with the Spirit, relying on God's power and perspective.

———————

To close this chapter, I want to share a story about my youngest son, Augustus, and his first revelation of the Holy Spirit.

When he was three, my older kids decided that we should watch a Nancy Drew movie for family night. Upon a quick review, the movie seemed innocent enough, and since I grew up reading the Hardy Boys, I've always been a sucker for tales of mystery. We made the popcorn, snuggled up on the couch, and began the film. Everything was going splendidly until we encountered a ghost roughly halfway through the film. When the spirit appeared, I tried to both cover Augustus's eyes and rationalize the fear. A confusing message, to be sure.

"Auggie, the ghost isn't real—this is the mystery that Nancy Drew will soon solve. You don't need to be afraid, buddy. See, the ghost didn't hurt her because it isn't real."

But I could tell by the look on his face that I had missed the mark. His eyes were big and his stare blank. No amount of rationalization would help—I had just created a ghost complex, and I knew it. I considered taking him out of the room but decided instead to let him finish the wild ride, hoping that

Nancy Drew would be her usual heroine self and explain away all the fear.

I'll spare you the details, but let's just say I spent the next six months navigating a host of questions on ghosts along with the occasional bouts of night-induced trauma. I felt terrible. My brave little boy was now afraid of the dark, all because I let him watch a stupid Nancy Drew movie. I couldn't help but wonder where this trauma would take him. I began imagining myself twenty years from now sitting with Augustus, who now has tired eyes and a beard, explaining this whole situation to a shrink who's charging us thousands of dollars to unfurl all the harm that I've done.

But just when I thought I was forever lost in *The Princess Bride*'s Pit of Despair, a ray of hope broke through the dark night: *Addison, introduce Augustus to the Holy Ghost.* That was it! Auggie's synaptic jungle wouldn't allow the ghost neurons to escape—the only solution was to take a *Jumanji*-like journey in and unveil a good God-ghost who could vanquish the bad ghosts.

I proceeded to explain the Holy Spirit to Augustus. Now, the Holy Spirit is hard enough to explain to adults. Even with my training in pneumatology, and the fact that I coauthored a book on the Holy Spirit, I found myself inadequate for the task at hand. Fear is, after all, a formidable foe—one that morphs, evolves, and ultimately feeds on the unknown. My words had no weight. They just slid out of my mouth only to collect in the valley of confusion that somehow grew wider with each attempt at clarity. This wasn't working.

But then, once again, the dawn of hope was awakened. Augustus's confused stare transformed into confident assurance. With a sanguine and almost cheeky smile, Augustus said, "The

Holy Ghost doesn't want to scare me, Dad, . . . the Holy Ghost wants to love me!"

I was blanked.

That's so simple. So perfect. Why didn't I say that? "Yes, Augustus—the Holy Ghost wants to love you!"

For you did not receive the spirit of slavery to fall back into fear, but you have received the Spirit . . . by whom we cry, "Abba! Father!" (Rom. 8:15)

In the words of my son, God's Spirit wants to love you. In his letter that we now know as 1 John, John repeatedly tells us that it is through the gift of God's Spirit that we can abide in the revelation of love.[14] Paul expresses a similar sentiment in his letter to the Romans: "God's love has been poured into our hearts through the Holy Spirit."[15] There it is. The Holy Ghost wants to love you; it's worth saying again.

And to take it a step further—not that I'm trying to one-up a three-year-old—the Holy Spirit wants to invite us into *perichōrēsis*, the divine love dance. The place where we're taught the art of integrative prayer. The place where we learn to hear the Voice.

8

I Am Here

So don't worry about tomorrow, for tomorrow will bring its own worries. Today's trouble is enough for today.

Matthew 6:34 NLT

Lead me to the heart of the present that I may be a sharer of your eternal presence.

John Philip Newell, *Sounds of the Eternal*

Have you ever spent time with someone who is profoundly present? A soul who can't help but give everything she has to the beauty and opportunity of each moment. These Saints seem to almost have a bit of mischief behind their eyes, like they're on the verge of telling a secret whose time is not yet come. There's a Latin word that was once used to describe such folk: *hilaritas*. Like its English counterparts, *hilarious* and *hilarity*, this Latin word conveys joy, excitement, celebration.

It's not that life is a big joke to these souls, nor is it that they're out of tune with the gravitas of existence; rather, it is because they are so in tune with the seriousness of each moment that they can't help but look life in the eyes only to see that it's usually smiling back at them.

The YOLO (you only live once) spirit of our age is a distortion of what I'm describing. Living under the weight of the concept eat, drink, and be merry for tomorrow we die leads only to premature death. One could say that reckless living leaves death to the Fates while the way of Life, in contrast, invites us to voluntarily lay down our lives, dying to the smallness of self *daily* so we can live in the reality of the kingdom. Only then can we defeat the Fates and choose death on our terms.

The problem is most of us don't know how to die while living, so we spend most of our lives as slaves to death, with fear—a fear rooted in self-preservation—as our primary guide. We forget, so it would seem, what Scripture says: "that through death he might destroy the one who has the power of death, that is, the devil, and deliver all those who through fear of death were subject to lifelong slavery."[1]

Perfect love casts out fear, and the Accuser can no longer hang death over our heads. When we die daily, we participate in God's redemptive purpose for death, and we see, with clarity, what really matters about any given moment and find the strength to live life to the fullest, receiving from and giving to life what is best.[2]

Nowhere is this truth more evident than in the presence of one who knows they have only days or hours to live. Life, as it truly is, becomes clear to them. Priorities line up differently; people become more forgivable; risk looks more tolerable; inaction feels more consequential; time is seen as less expendable.

And with this lucidity, most of us can work out what to do, when to do it, and with whom we must do it.

But must we wait until then? Whether we have decades or days to live, is there a way to bring death's clarity into this very moment?

The answer is yes.

But the yes, like all good yeses, comes with a cost.

Most of us spend our lives living anywhere but the present, and the enemy of our soul likes it that way. Based on research done by Matthew A. Killingsworth and Daniel T. Gilbert of Harvard University, people spend nearly half their waking hours thinking about the nonpresent or disengaged from what they're doing. "How often our minds leave the present and where they tend to go," writes Killingsworth, "is a better predictor of our happiness than the activities in which we are engaged."[3]

In the middle of his teaching on kingdom living, not long after teaching us how to pray, Jesus shares this same truth. Before you read it, stop a moment and invite God to talk to you through this passage. Sit in silence. Breathe in and out. Close your eyes for a minute, then as you open them, begin to read.

> Therefore I tell you, do not be anxious about your life, what you will eat or what you will drink, nor about your body, what you will put on. Is not life more than food, and the body more than clothing? Look at the birds of the air: they neither sow nor reap nor gather into barns, and yet your heavenly Father feeds them. Are you not of more value than they? And which of you by being anxious can add a single hour to his span of life? And why are you anxious about clothing? Consider the lilies

of the field, how they grow: they neither toil nor spin, yet I tell you, even Solomon in all his glory was not arrayed like one of these. But if God so clothes the grass of the field, which today is alive and tomorrow is thrown into the oven, will he not much more clothe you, O you of little faith? Therefore do not be anxious, saying, "What shall we eat?" or "What shall we drink?" or "What shall we wear?" For the Gentiles seek after all these things, and your heavenly Father knows that you need them all. But seek first the kingdom of God and his righteousness, and all these things will be added to you.

Therefore do not be anxious about tomorrow, for tomorrow will be anxious for itself. Sufficient for the day is its own trouble. (Matt. 6:25–34)

I don't need to define *anxiety* because chances are you know it better than you'd like to. Anxiety is what happens to us when we try to live in the future, when we try to supersede chronology's limitations and insert ourselves in another place or time.

Like the old joke goes, "Start worrying. Details to follow."

We give ourselves over to worry when we face a moment that is not yet ours to face. That is why faith is so important; it is the antidote to worry. If faith is the substance of things hoped for, then worry is the substance of that which we dread. Faith is power. Worry is anti-power. Faith brings clarity. Worry delivers confusion. Faith begets action. Worry creates inaction. Faith gives us eyes for the moment. Worry blinds us to the sacred now.

The moment you are in is too important to ignore, for everything happens in the Eternal Now. And that is why Jesus tells us not to be anxious or worry. Give those cares to the One who cares for you. He's not saying that the cares aren't important. What we eat, where we go, what we do, who we love—these things are, in fact, too important for your ignorance, their weight too heavy for you to carry. The Father delights in every detail of your life, and not just your life: even the life of grass, "which today is alive and tomorrow is thrown into the oven," won't escape his notice or care.

The only way to see this moment's true form, which is wrapped in the ultimate reality of God's kingdom, is to seek it as a beloved child:

Truly, I say to you, unless you turn and become like children, you will never enter the kingdom of heaven. (Matt. 18:3)

And,

Let the children come to me, and do not hinder them, for to such belongs the kingdom of God. (Luke 18:16)

It is here that we should call out three qualities of beloved children.

First, they expect to find what they are looking or asking for. My kids' audacity amazes me. Their faith in me as a dad straight-up scares me sometimes. Whether that's them encouraging me to jump and fly off the roof or make all of them different meals in ten minutes, they expect results, and I love it (except when I don't).

Second, they know the world is bigger than what they've seen. Think back to when you were a child, reach to those memories of adventures you used to have in the backyard or the basement. There was an unspoken expectation that what you imagined— that person, place, or thing—could become real. And the adventure was energized by the "impossible" becoming possible. You weren't in search of a small space to conquer. The truth of life wasn't something you systematized and controlled, it was something that you wandered into through play, pain, and joy. At some point, all of us go from being explorers to controllers, trading mystery for misery. The kingdom's ultimate reality, however, requires us to let go of what we can grasp, allowing ourselves to be grasped by what seems greater than us, yet is somehow more truly us.

Third, they are intimate with the present moment. I think this attribute helps explain why kids are so resilient. They can handle whatever life throws at them because children take life one moment at a time. If we're honest about our lives, things are rarely as horrible as we thought they would be. Yet how much energy is lost worrying about challenges that are not ours to face yet? How would your life change if you only used today's energy to face off with today's cares? If I'm honest, I'm overcome by a day only when I've brought other days into the mix.

In a way it's hard to believe that what I write is true, but we know it to be so.

Another good question to ask yourself is, Has worry or anxiety ever helped me get what I want or need? There are, of course, redemptive benefits from failing and learning from our failures, but for our purposes, let's just evaluate the effectiveness of worry itself.

Over the course of a few years, I, figuring conservatively, traded more than a thousand hours of sleep for nocturnal worry and anxiety. I can honestly say that trade was entirely ineffective, except to teach me just how useless worry is. By the time I'd get out of bed, hundreds of concerns, both imminent and distant, had crossed my mind, so it would feel as if I had already navigated a day or two or ten, and I had very little strength to navigate the real cares and challenges that the day would inevitably bring.

I justified my stupidity by listening to the voice that constantly told me I must try harder and do more, otherwise I would never be enough, and my future would fall apart. This lie became a stronghold in my life, and I couldn't see any Truth beyond its walls. People would tell me to trust God and cast my cares on him, but I didn't really know what that meant. I would never have said it like this, but I guess I just believed that that was a nice thing people who don't have weighty responsibilities could cling to—my pride justified by the belief that I was suffering for the people who depended on me . . . and for God.

In Psalm 127 we're told that God, not us, is the master builder of our lives. When we forget this truth, we trade meaningful work for vain effort. According to Solomon, the psalm's author, "it is in vain that you rise up early and go late to rest, eating the bread of anxious toil."[4] Notice that anxiety does offer a type of sustenance ("the bread of anxious toil"). In other words, in a twisted way, anxiety both feeds and starves us. It feeds us the lie that we are self-sufficient, while starving us from the sustenance of godly satisfaction. If we are to taste the daily manna, the Father's heavenly bread (a Hebrew word that literally means "What is it?"), we must let go of the anxiety that comes with being in control, for all suffering is caused by an unmet desire for control.

The Father has a way of not delivering us from something when he knows that thing will ultimately deliver us to him. He is patient in and with our pain, willing to suffer alongside us for the joy ahead. For what good father does not share in the pain of his child? The mystery of Immanuel, God with us, was made known through the Son's life, and his Spirit works in us to make us more aware of God's closeness. I once heard Scripture described as a progression of our ability to comprehend God's union with us. In the Old Testament, God was known as the One who was *for* his people; he would fight for them, but, so it would seem, remain at arm's length.

God for us.

And then Jesus entered the scene. Taking on flesh, God looked a lot like us. He walked our roads, ate our food, cried our tears, spilled our blood. The transcendent God became an imminent presence, the holiness of his presence joining itself to every person and space. In truth, nothing was off-limits to Jesus—sinner and Sadducee, temple and tomb, oppressor and oppressed. Jesus was the evidence of the beautiful and terrifying truth that God is with us, willing to go wherever he is welcomed.

God with us.

But God's revelation of selfhood didn't stop with an example. Instead, the Spirit moved into our very selves, redefining any notion of temple, worship, and family; breaking down the secular/sacred divides that create an illusion that there are parts of our lives or work that are off-limits to God or beyond his care. If Jesus had remained among us, we wouldn't have matured into the awareness that God is within us. "It is better for you that I go away." In his absence we are forced to seek out why and how our lives are linked with his, our every inhale the exhale of God's eternal breath.

God within us.

––––––––

Freedom from time's tyranny is found only in the present. When we are slaves to the past, we're overcome with regret. When we are slaves to the future, we're undermined by anxiety. The reason for this is simple. Aside from the Spirit's guidance, we are not able to simultaneously function in the past, present, and future. God is the only one who gets to inhabit eternity, the One who was and is and will be. We, on the other hand, are called to be faithful with the day, this moment, releasing our past to God while trusting him with our future. When we let our minds wander into the nonpresent, it's as if we eat from the Tree of Knowledge of Good and Evil, and our lives break down. Our attempts to live outside the present are an attempt to circumvent God and his ways. It is idolatry. And anytime we give ourselves over to idolatry—that notion that we can somehow manufacture our own sense of godhood—whether our god is internal or external, our lives fall apart. But here's the amazing, upside-down truth: when we are faithful (full of faith) with the day, the Voice offers insight that leads to foresight. Through faith we participate in the Eternal Now. It is not a look into the future. It is a look into an eternal present.

> Fight the good fight of the faith. Take hold of the *eternal life* to which you were called. (1 Tim. 6:12, emphasis mine)

Notice that faith isn't a supernatural ability to escape the day. I often hear faith described as the power to conform the world to our own liking, a way for us to bend the material world to what we perceive as highest and best, relieving ourselves of the kingdom responsibility that stands right before us. But faith isn't an escape from the present moment, it is a plunge into the heart of a moment so we can see the moment for what it truly is. In that place of radical trust—a trust that grows as we believe there is no moment too dark or mountain too high, that God's presence shall not be contained—we become unshakable. It is only when we believe that some hardship or person can separate us from God's presence that we lose touch with Truth.

The mountain-moving faith of Scripture is the power that's native to the will and reality of God. You could say that faith is the launchpad for a different point of view, a new perspective of "knowing" itself. Regardless of what or who stands in our way, God can reshape the moment, but only if we are honest with the moment. Only if the moment has our absolute attention, for that is what faith is: the absolute attention to what is most real and a refusal to relent until such knowledge covers the earth like the waters cover the seas.

So, in essence, we see the past and future *through* the day, rather than around it. This is how we learn from our past and plan for our future without falling into regret or anxiety. God loves redeeming what was and readying us for what will be. He's not trying to put blinders on our eyes or keep us from being people of vision. We need hope, which is vision, to flourish in life. We become visionaries, however, not by escaping the moment but by being radically present to it.

When I am tempted to circumvent the day, I simply pray, *Father, when I face that moment, whatever the moment may be, I ask that you give me the wisdom to know what to do and the grace to do it.* This prayer, while simple, is effective for multiple reasons.

First, it doesn't belittle the gravity of whatever is weighing on my mind. It doesn't require that I participate in a nontruth; rather, it invites me to surrender to the greater truth that God promises me wisdom and grace. Wisdom, for me, is defined as knowing what to do. People who operate in the gift of wisdom see harmony where others see only contradiction; wise people enter messes only to emerge as conciliatory messengers, bringing principle, people, and process together in ways that were previously undiscernible.

What makes the wise so effective is their comfort with para-dox. They fear God and thus refuse to make light of what is beyond them. In humility, they find grace, which is the infu-sion of the Divine, to see, feel, and act beyond their limita-tions. One could say they harmonize with a greater wisdom that integrates their life experience, the problem at hand, and a universal consciousness that is the mind of Christ. This is the wisdom of the Saints and mystics, the ones who fight the world's attempts to reduce everything to dualities and violence. Such wisdom isn't just reserved for the navigating of nations or the leading of companies, it belongs in the most mundane interactions, the nooks and crannies of everyday life—for what is often judged as commonplace is what's most vital to human flourishing.

Second, this little prayer shoos concerns back to their proper place and time. Concerns that are prone to chronological wan-derings have a way of taking on monstrous forms, and the only way to expose them for what they truly are is to face them when their designated time comes. We all know that the idea of a thing is normally more terrifying than the thing itself. This truth is so universal that I don't even need to provide an anecdote, for you know it to be true. But still, in our attempts for control, we try to tackle more than what is necessary for the day, and our lives start to shudder and shake, our feet made heavy by the weight of our idols.

Too often we attach our peace to the outcome of a certain event: an election, a marriage, a child, a diagnosis, the list goes on. But as life teaches us again and again, there is always something beyond the thing: another mountain to climb, an-other valley to cross, another sea to forge. Thomas M. Sterner writes,

There is almost always this sense that something needs to change in our life in order for everything to be just right. No matter what we accomplish or acquire, this feeling has a way of contaminating what we are experiencing now.[5]

Sterner challenges us to ask the simple question "And then what?" So you graduate college . . . and then what? You get married . . . and then what? You have kids . . . and then what? You get that job . . . and then what? You start a company . . . and then what? You fail . . . and then what?

Many of us feel defined by what we do, so it's natural for us to obsess over what we'll do when *that event* happens. But life is more than a series of things to be done. As children of God, what we do is significant, but only insofar as it prepares us for what is behind the task. The task itself is not the goal; the goal is what is forged in us through the task. Most of what we build with our hands will pass away, but our formation is of eternal value, creating a foundation for a different dimension of work and stewardship in the age to come.

As we close this chapter, I want to leave you with another practical prayer, something that I use to engage with the moment at hand. I primarily use this prayer during my morning routine, to prepare my heart for a time of *lectio divina*, a term from the Benedictine tradition that means a contemplative reading of Scripture. This type of reading is not an attempt to master or subdue the text to one's desired aims or needs of that moment; rather, it is a yielding to the text, allowing Scripture to read us.

This prayer is simple but robust, consisting of three words that form three pathways for my soul to surrender to.

I am here.

The first pathway is a surrender of place. Since I am not God, I am not omnipresent. Since I am *here*, I cannot be there, whatever there is: a phone call, a message, a meeting, a project. Here is where I am, and I surrender to this space. I cannot be two places at once, and we all know how bad we are at multitasking, regardless of how hard we try to convince ourselves otherwise.

I am here.

The second pathway is a surrender of time. Since I am not God, I am bound by time's constraints. For me, this prayer is a yielding of where I think I should be. When my soul is led by my insecurities, I hardly ever feel like I'm what I should be as a son, father, brother, writer, leader, friend—you name it. When I pray, *I am here*, I am challenged to thank God for the good and patient work he has done in me, while dying to my ideas of where I should be. There's nothing wrong with being critical of our progress, but there's certainly a right manner and method to pursue.

I am here.

The third pathway is a surrender of reality. The great I AM is in fact here with me, in this moment. There's so much talk about self-awareness, but true self-awareness only follows God-awareness. When we are not gripped by the holiness of God and the reality that we are his children, Saints (holy ones), children of the Holy One, our awareness is hampered at best and entirely distorted at worst. It's only in the light of surrender that we find eyes to see the One who cannot be seen. In other words, we cannot systematize a pathway of illumination, for how do we grasp what can only grasp us? Rather, we must wander into his worthiness, trusting that repentance, which is nothing less than an acknowledgment of blindness, will lead to the ability to see, know, and obey.

We can be here.

Paul once wrote to the Saints in Philippi, "Let your reasonableness be known to everyone. The Lord is at hand; do not be anxious about anything."[6] For Paul, the only way one could be reasonable (also translated "gentle") in this life is by living in the reality that the *Lord is at hand*.

The idiom *at hand* conveys two important truths: first, that the person is near; second, that the person is able to do something about your situation. Paul can write that "the Lord is at hand" only if both conditions are met.

When we are people of the present, we can participate in the reality of God's presence. The Lord is at hand with and within us as we travel through every moment. Life is not something we just get through, while making sure we pray the right prayer and not mess up too badly—all for the purpose of getting to heaven when we die.

Life is something we can get caught up in now and live in forever. It is only then that we become the kind of people, in this present time, that the world needs. The Saints found in Hebrews 11 were profoundly present and in tune with what God was doing because they could see the unseen. Through faith they didn't run from the tension between *what is* and *what should be*. They didn't hide from the dissonance around them. They saw both a heavenly city and their earthly location, refusing to let go of either reality, while submitting the lesser reality to the greater. Such a radical demonstration made them both people the world wasn't worthy of and exactly what the world needed.

They disrupted, in a good way, a chain of events that set the stage for the perfect expression of God's true nature and purpose: Jesus.

Our soul is restless until it finds its rest in God.[7] There is always something more. Something other. Something lacking. Some opportunity. Some care. And that's not a bad thing. In this age, we are made strong through weakness, perfect through imperfection, whole through brokenness, rooted through storms. Don't believe the lie that prayer is supposed to deliver you from this moment; God intends for prayer to deliver you *through* this moment. When the miracle comes—and it will come, for everything that is now "impossible" has an end date—will you have eyes to see your deliverance? Will you know the nature of your deliverer? Will you find your rest in God?

The great I AM is here. He always has been and always will be.

Oh God, give us eyes to see that even now, we are living in an answered prayer.

9

How Should We Ask?

You do not have, because you do not ask.

James 4:2

God wishes to give himself utterly to every creature that names his name.

Jeanna Guyon, *Experiencing the Depths of Jesus Christ*

Why do we need to pray to a God who is all-powerful and all-knowing? If something of the good sort needs to get done, won't the good Father tend to it, whether we ask him to or not?

Before you throw a Christian cliché back at me, sit with these questions—make both the questions and answers personal.

Even Jesus told us to keep our prayers short and sweet, for the Father knows what we need before we ask.[1] If the Father does indeed know what we need, then why does Scripture encourage us to ask for bread and mountains to move?

One of the paradoxes of our Father's kingdom is that he invites us to relentlessly ask *for what we need* while cultivating contentment *with what we have.*

If the Lord's Prayer is to be followed, we, based on Jesus's own words, ask the Father for what he already knows we need. Sometimes I wonder if anyone else has struggled with this paradox. I'd rather it be one or the other: either give me what I specifically ask for in prayer or grant me the release to just pray, "Your will be done." But if we're honest about Jesus's example, we know that we don't get the luxury of either/or. We must, once again, embrace the tension of non-dual thinking. As Jesus modeled in the garden, with blood leaking from his pores, we must be *specific* ("let this cup pass"), *surrendered* ("not my will but yours be done"), and *steadfast* (he prayed these words three times).

In fact, any great prayer is one that is specific, surrendered, and steadfast. All three of these dimensions are essential and cannot be marginalized.

Whether our prayer is a bold ask or simple surrender, it must be anything but vague. The Father can do a lot with an imperfect prayer, but a vague prayer doesn't do much for anyone. A large part of bringing our requests to the Father is that it creates opportunity for us to better understand his nature. In Luke 11, we're told that God responds to our prayerful petitions because of the honor of his name, and he gives us even more than what we ask for.[2] He is Jehovah Jireh, the God who provides, and it is our petitions that help open our eyes to the reality of who he is.

In my childhood I encountered a church stream that was rather fond of asking God for stuff. In fact, it seemed like the people who were celebrated and platformed were those who would ask for and receive things from God. These testimonies of material gain—houses, cars, planes, boats, money, and so on—were used to build the congregation's faith and inspire more giving. The spirit of it all never sat right with me. It seemed like people were using select Scriptures to get the hottest goods on the market, indulging their selfishness and greed while calling their actions holy.

I could not have articulated it back then as I can now, but what troubled me was that the emphasis on the material gains seemed to confuse the focus of worship. God was given glory for these things, but it sure seemed like the glory was in the stuff itself. Put off by what I saw, I shied away from asking God for anything unless that "thing" was super noble or for someone else. Over time, however, I noticed that much of my prayer life had become vague and impersonal, even when I was asking on behalf of others. It felt as if my spirit was blocked, as if I were denying myself a power and perspective that percolates only as we bring real, tangible requests to the Father.

I was missing it.

An anti-response is not normally the right response. Merely running in the opposite direction of a lie does not necessarily lead us to the Father's house of Truth. The question we must all ask ourselves is not "Is it wrong for them?" but rather "What must I do?" Religion has a way of obsessing over the wrongness of others, distracting us from the interior work that is wrought only through our own self-awareness and obedience. As Paul instructed Timothy, we should possess or take care of our own souls; once we do that, the Father has a way of entrusting us with the souls of others.[3] Or as Jesus put it, that brother of yours does indeed have a speck in his eye, and we all know what a nasty thing it is to have something in our eyes, but you cannot serve your brother and remove the speck if you will not first acknowledge your own log, the one that is blinding you to anything other than a projection of your own pain and disappointment.

Around the time I was learning to bring requests to God again—for I think most of us once knew how to ask and have since forgotten—my wife and I moved into our first house. We were so excited to finally have a home with a yard and such. Our new space was nearly twice as large as our previous spot, and with more square footage came more cost. We leveraged most of our cash to get into the house, so there wasn't much in our reserves for outfitting the place. We were blissfully house poor. Juli and I knew we would have to be patient and intentional with our spending and allowed the challenge to ignite our creativity, making our efforts to turn a house into our home especially meaningful.

We moved into our Colorado home in February, and if you know Colorado, you know that nothing grows there in February. Our place did have a small piece of grass in the backyard, though, that would eventually need to be mowed. As spring drew closer, I started to think about my lawn mower. There was some green in the grass, and I knew my time was coming. But the patch of grass was small, and we still didn't have a sofa to sit on. And there was also the fact that we had met a neighbor with a great lawn mower who would surely lend me his for the five minutes it would take me to mow our little patch of green.

But I really wanted a lawn mower. So I took a trip to Lowe's . . . just to look around.

Of course, the lawn mowers were on full display, parading their power. After circling the selection like a lion after a gazelle,

I convinced myself that I should take the plunge and purchase a lawn mower. Sure, Juli probably wouldn't understand, but I could find a way to make things right with her . . . right?

Then a strange thing happened to me. Out of nowhere—and I mean nowhere!—I heard the Spirit of God tell me, *Ask me to give you a lawn mower.* The Voice was so clear that I couldn't deny what I had heard. Plus, I should mention that I'm awful at receiving things from people, so I knew the idea wasn't mine. So I took a deep breath, and simply asked God to give me a lawn mower. With my eyes drifting back to what could've been mine, I left Lowe's, a bit confused by it all.

Within days, I think it was three days later, I received a call from a friend whom I hadn't spoken to in almost a year. I'm not great about answering calls, but for some reason I knew this one needed to be answered. There was a bit of the usual small talk, and my friend told me that he and his family were moving to Florida soon. He then casually mentioned that he had a lawn mower that he couldn't bring with him and wanted to know if I wanted it.

I was speechless.

After recovering myself, I asked him how much he'd sell it for. "Nothing," he responded. Then he told me that he was planning to sell it but felt a nudge to call me and offer it to me first. I almost started crying. The whole thing probably felt a bit clumsy to him. I mean, it was a great gift, but the way I responded you would've thought I had just been offered the car or house of my dreams. For me, of course, it was not the lawn mower itself. The lawn mower, like any other thing, is just a thing. My excitement gushed from a deep knowing that my life would never be the same. A facet of the Father's character and faithfulness became real to me that day, and I knew, like I knew my name was Addison, that our requests, and God's response to them, are an intimate and necessary part of our formation as sons and daughters.

––––––––

Right in the heart of the Lord's Prayer, we are instructed to ask for bread. Matthew and Luke differ in their version of The Prayer, but both accounts make it clear that God cares for our provision and encourages us to look to him for it.

The idea of bread does, of course, extend beyond literal bread. It includes everything that sustains the life God has given to us. It is through this bread that we find strength to participate in God's will and kingdom that is to be revealed in our lives and work. Remember that moment when Jesus told his disciples that he had food that they knew not of? He was speaking of the nourishment of being in step with what matters most, of feasting at the table of blessed kingdom work. There is a pure joy that comes with knowing what is to be done and doing it, and Jesus knew in full what we've known only in part.

For a child to grow in stature, they must receive regular sustenance; otherwise, their growth will be stunted, their health compromised, and their capacity limited. When it comes to matters of the kingdom, daily bread is where the kingdom takes on flesh. It is the convergence of the transcendent and imminent, the supranatural and natural, the material and mystical. This moment in the Lord's Prayer undermines our tendency to draw clean lines around the secular and sacred, separating them for our own pleasure and purposes. Even our daily grind is holy and part of God's good work. A truth that can be tasted in the bread of our blood, sweat, and tears. A bread that, like the loaves and fishes, multiplies as it is blessed, broken, and shared.

We ask for daily bread so we can know we're living in an answered prayer. Every day, the miraculous surrounds us, and it is our surrendered "ask" that helps *us* connect the dots. We ask to become aware, and only those who ask are aware. This is the sort of truth that Jesus is getting at when he says to those who have, more will be given.[4] As Tertullian put it, "We are asking that we should perpetually be in Christ and that we should not be separated from his body."[5] He is the vine, and we are the branches.[6] The fruit of our life matters to him because it is his, and our lives abound in and with sustenance as we realize that our life source owns the cattle on a thousand hills.

At the beginning of this chapter, I quoted James's famous words: "You do not have, because you do not ask." Well, I think it could also be said that *you know not what you have because you do not ask*. How can you know that the Father cares for your sustenance if you won't ask him to sustain you?

A month or so ago a friend of mine and I were talking about different miracles that we've seen, miracles tied to the idea of asking for bread. He shared a story about a time when he and his dad lived in Mexico, and they had nothing in the refrigerator and no money to buy groceries. The plan was to go to bed hungry. But my friend told his dad that they should pray and ask God for pizza and Pepsi, and so they did. A few minutes later, a neighbor knocked on the door of their apartment and offered them, you guessed it, pizza and Pepsi.

I realize God doesn't always provide the way we expect him to. A miracle is what happens when an outcome outpaces our expectation, and God tends to move slower than we'd like.

But the Father is not put off by our asks. In fact, we are told to approach the throne of grace boldly. The word that Jesus uses for prayerful asks, *aiteo*, conveys a boldness or temerity. It is even translated "demand" at times. We are charged to ask expecting a response. Now the response may not be exactly what we expected. Scripture tells us that the Father retains the right to refuse and will not give us stones, scorpions, and serpents.[7] There are times, in our limited understanding, when we think we're asking for bread or fish (something that sustains and grows us) but we're really asking for stones and snakes (things that weigh us down and destroy us). But here's the thing: it is often through asking for the wrong that we learn to distinguish between stones and bread, fish and snakes. For the persistent ones, the ones who consistently bring their petitions to God, the tension of getting it wrong is formative to their ability to get it right.

We learn to ask correctly only through asking . . . and can we even value what we haven't learned to ask for?

For the most part, we do a good job encouraging kids to be inquisitive during the early years, and this is a large part of their rapid growth. But at some point, maybe because we're annoyed, tired, or just lacking sufficient answers, we start to discourage their asks. Phrases like "Because I said so" or "That's just how things are" or "No!" become default responses, and eventually children look to other sources for their answers, or they stop asking altogether—viewing the ask itself as a sign of their ignorance, a blinking light that lets the world know that we've got a slow one here.

In Jewish culture, the ability to ask good questions is a sign of maturity. In fact, it is the primary responsibility of the parents to teach their children how to ask questions, to inquire into the unsure.[8] It is by making requests and asking questions that we venture into the connectedness of all things, an element of

God's kingdom reality. This is scary business, but it is good and necessary for us to wrestle with what is ultimately true.

Because asking is risky, many of us prefer the safety of not putting ourselves out there, of not knowing what's on the other side of a request. With very little tolerance for rejection, we shrink into ourselves, hoping that everything we need lies within our own sufficiency. But here's the thing: self-sufficiency is an illusion, for The Prayer tells us that we must ask for even something as simple as bread. There is nothing we have that the Father hasn't given us, and the sooner we get to asking the sooner we realize that.

The request, though, isn't just about us—our needs, desires, sufficiency (or lack thereof). We are instructed to ask for each other. Give *us* this day *our* daily bread. Once again, we're confronted with prayer's integrating power. Our requests represent much more than our individual selves.

When bringing our requests to the Father, Jesus tells us to allow the first movement of The Prayer to restore us to wonder. Any request for our daily bread follows a meditation on God's character, presence, and purpose. When we don't follow the sequence in The Prayer, we're tempted to believe the lie that the world and its problems are more real and greater than our Father in the heavens. Taking time to dwell in God's domain, if you will, prepares us to return to our own. But as we return to the material world, we notice that we pray in a company of Saints, a revelation that emboldens and enlarges our requests.

As N. T. Wright puts it, "The danger with the prayer for bread is that we get there too soon."[9] If you think about it, most people begin a prayer with something that you'd find at the middle or end of the Lord's Prayer: deliver me from this hardship, avenge me, give me what I need. I'm not knocking such prayers. After all, any genuine, imperfect request has a way of kick-starting a perfect process in our lives. But prayer makes a whole lot more sense when we acknowledge the domain and authority of the One we're praying to. If God is indeed our Father and his nature supersedes any distinction of time or place, then we know he can and will participate in our real needs, feeding us as he does the sparrows.

But what about requests that go unanswered? What about those who lack their daily bread? These are not easy questions to answer, nor can there be an answer that captures the whole truth.

I will respond, though, that we must remember that this lifetime, when compared to the timelessness of eternity, is a vapor. Bound by time, our struggles in this life can feel unfair and final. But we are told that our prayers touch both heaven and earth. There is a resonance among the dimensions, even if time and space keep us from seeing it. Sometimes the resonance is clear and visible to us, like the pizza and Pepsi, but there will be many requests whose nature (and answer) will be known only in the awareness of eternity. I do believe that through communion with God's eternal Spirit, though, we can receive answers in the heart that cannot always be articulated with the mouth, a reason why praying with our heart is such an important part of our prayer life.

The Father promises, however, that our requests do their work, even when there's no visible resonance. That is why we must keep asking and contending. Heaven and earth are connected in our prayers. Jesus tells us so. Moses wanted to go into the Promised Land but was denied entrance. Yet we find him 1,300 years later standing in the Promised Land with the Son, transfigured in glory.

When I prayed for Ivan to be healed from cancer, I believed that he would be healed. I asked that he'd have ten more years, yet he didn't. But the Spirit has shown me things about Ivan and his life that transcend time. God worked through Ivan's life to impact so many lives and continues to do so through his family, friends, my family, and even this book.

I would also add that we, as the children of our Father, have a responsibility to offer sustenance to each other. God wants us to participate in the joyful work of his kingdom, which includes taking care of each other. The breaking of bread and sharing what they had was a central part of the early church's identity and effectiveness.

Toward the end of his life, King David wrote that he had never seen the righteous forsaken or their children begging for bread.[10] He goes on to say that the righteous are generous with what they have. Another way to say that is they live under the banner of "our bread." When the righteous understand that everything belongs to the Father, not just their "tithe," they open their eyes to what stewardship requires of them.

Bringing our requests to the Father is another way of saying yes to him and his process.

Prayer is much more than a transaction; it's a transformative journey into the Father's heart. There is so much the Father wants to give us through prayer, but he is not Santa Claus, dropping gifts to the names that escaped the naughty list. The gift is himself, not something that he or some magical creature created in a distant workshop. With every request, new threads are woven into the tapestry of our transformation, and these threads, while seemingly insignificant for a time, capture every moment of pain and longing, so that nothing goes wasted or forgotten. When the time comes, and come it shall, we will receive our request as part of ourselves, a point of intimate connection between the Father's nature and our own.

Have you ever seen the movie *Evan Almighty*, starring Steve Carell and Morgan Freeman? The movie itself may be worth only a single watch, but I do love how a specific prayer is answered as the movie takes shape. Toward the beginning of the movie, the mom, whose family is clearly growing apart, prays that her family would grow closer together. She expects, as we all do at times, for God to simply give them all butterflies and warm feelings toward each other. What she doesn't realize is that if God were to do that, he would be imposing his will on them, denying them the chance to choose what is better and best.

Instead of growing closer together, the family is shaken apart and collapses. But in the collapse, the old, broken family dynamic dies, and a new family, if you will, emerges. The old quirks are still there, but the family is grounded in a purpose and connection that create space for the idiosyncrasies and differences that previously drove them apart.

Often, we think our petitions will flatten the landscape of our lives, leading to a more predictable, comfortable, or manageable existence. But prayer doesn't work like that. As we learn to pray, life has a way of becoming more beautifully dangerous. We see more. Feel more. Hear more. Participate in more. The ostensible comfort that comes with living inside our small sense of self is seen for the neurosis that it is. Don't get me wrong, God holds us in his hand and promises a safety that cannot be shaken. But this safety mustn't be the meticulous work of our own designs (or prayers). The safety is found in knowing that wherever our request may take us, God, too, will be there, holding us by the hand.

The safety is in surrender.

The safety *is* surrender.

Every ask leads to an adventure.

Bring your specific requests to the Father. They are important to him; a request is a holy thing. But pray *through* each one by releasing them to the Father. When we entrust each petition to the Father, placing it in his loving hands, we are no longer weighed down by the request's burden and can see what's on the other side of each ask, for the petition itself is not ultimate. There will always be another request.

In any moment, a request or two may dominate our consciousness, keeping us from seeing anything beyond its fulfillment. When we are starving, it's hard to think of anything beyond our next meal. Once the hunger abates, however, there is a world of needs and wants that line up for our attention. When we hunger and thirst after righteousness, we feed on heavenly bread, a bread that sustains our struggle for temporal needs and desires. The temporal is not unholy, for even it, in a way, belongs to the eternal. Our longings prepare us for the love and wholeness (shalom) of the age to come. But when we allow the temporal need, a problem that surely has an end date, to blind us to the permanence of God's nature and promise, we lose the perspective that we need to ask with clarity and confidence, knowing that the present disconnect, whatever it may be, prepares us for perpetual glory.

Prayer is so powerful that God must retain the right to grant certain requests within our desired time line. But the moment a prayer leaves our lips, it begins its work. There is no prayer that goes unheard, but for our sake, there are prayers that must go unanswered. But no prayers, even the "bad" ones, are without purpose. Even a wrong step is better than no step, and the truth is, every finite step, in the light of God's infinite wisdom, is a less-than-perfect step. So run to the Father, or away from him if you must, but for heaven's sake, don't stand still. God has a way of guiding people who move their feet.

10

Confession, Sin, and Conscience

Search me, O God, and know my heart!
Try me and know my thoughts!
And see if there be any grievous way in me,
and lead me in the way everlasting!

Psalm 139:23–24

If you realize that in relation to God man is always wrong, your wrong may turn out to be right.

Paul Tillich, *The New Being*

When he was about eight, my son Asher started confessing his sins to me. Nearly every day a private audience would be requested, a time when Asher could share his misdeeds from the day. This would usually happen around bedtime, when his mind would catalogue that day's events and choose the ones that could morph into sleep stealers. When some deed felt especially heavy or heinous, he wouldn't wait until bedtime but would corner me as soon as I was home from work.

We would talk about what he had done, why he had done it, and work through what he was feeling in that moment. Asher had (and has) a strong sense of duty and a moral compass that borders on rigidity, so I spent most of our sessions affirming his desire to do what was right while exposing and confronting the pitfall of shame. We would talk, sometimes pray together, and that was the end of it.

Around this time, bedtime at our house required a deep breath. We had three kids in one room and a newborn in the other room. Juli did such a good job sleep training our kids when they were young, but I corrupted the routine as they got older. I couldn't refuse one more kiss, or glass of water, or song, or book. Eventually, my kids figured out they could delay bed-time and got remarkably good at figuring out things that they absolutely needed just as the lights went off.

There was a certain night, during this season, when bedtime proved to be especially difficult and drawn out. But I prevailed and the house was silent, which meant Juli and I were on our way to a quiet evening together. As I walked away from the room, though, the Holy Spirit nudged me to go get Asher out of bed and read to him for a bit. "Get behind me, Satan," was my first response; I wasn't about to disturb the peace that I had fought so hard for. But the nudge wouldn't go away.

After some delay, a delay that I hoped would give Asher more time to fall asleep, I snuck back into the room to see if he was still awake. Sure enough, he was, so I furtively removed Asher from the room without waking the other two kids, a miracle in itself.

Asher was delighted and shocked that I was taking him out of the room. Still questioning it all, I led him to the sofa, book in hand. But before a single word left my lips, Asher said, "Dad, can I tell you something?" I put the book down and said, "Absolutely."

"I said some bad words today."

"Really? Which ones?"

"*Stupid.*"

"Did you call someone stupid?"

"No, I just said the word."

"That's okay, Asher. Words are just sounds. It's what they mean to you or communicate to others that matters. Does that make sense?"

Asher looked as if the weight of the world was no longer on his back.

"Thanks, Dad. I also said . . ."

I couldn't believe what came next. My son dropped the most colorful series of f-bomb combos, one combination that I hadn't even heard before. The moment was so absurd that I almost lost my wits and burst out laughing. He had no idea what he was saying! The way he had set it all up made it clear that, to him, *stupid* was the bad word. These f-bombs were just a footnote in his confession.

"Asher," I finally responded, "where did you learn *that* word?"

Mortified, he looked at me for a couple seconds, trying to discern the word's severity, and then he broke down in tears, exclaiming, "The Holy Spirit told me it was a bad word after I said it. I'm sorry, Dad. I had no idea what it meant." I held him, and we talked about language and words, and where the f-word came from. I also asked him where he heard the word, even though I knew the answer.

That afternoon he had played with a boy in our neighborhood who lived with his mom and stepdad. The boy had a strained relationship with his stepdad, and I got the sense that he would repurpose and share harsh words to attract attention from the other kids. I really liked the kid and wanted Asher to be friends with him, but this new vocabulary wasn't ideal.

I told Asher that I needed to talk to the boy's mom. Asher wasn't excited about that. "Please, Dad, don't do that—anything but that!" After listening to his plea, I suggested that we both pray and ask the Spirit what we should do. Within ninety seconds or so, Asher spoke up: "Dad, the Holy Spirit told me that it's important for Ryan's future that you talk with his mom." I just sat there, stunned by his response. We prayed together, and then I walked him back to bed.

As I was leaving the room, the Spirit asked me, *Why do you think Asher confesses these things to you?* By that point, I was drained and ready to be done with it all, but I stopped and thought about it. The truth was, I had never taught Asher to confess. It was something that he initiated.

"Father, I don't know. Maybe he just doesn't like having things on his chest?"

That's true, son, but why does he confess to you?

"Because he feels safe with me."

Go deeper.

"Because I'm his father."

Yes. And because you're his father, he knows that you have the right to remind him of who he is, and he feels safe with you, knowing that he is "fiercely loved, not fiercely judged."[1]

Oh, I thought, *so this is what confession is all about . . .*

149

————

A prayer of confession has, for many, become a transaction, something that clears the ledger. There's a sense that God can forgive only what is confessed, so we rack our brains, searching out any wrong done or right left undone. Once every item is confessed we can be on our way, hopefully feeling bad enough to never do those things again.

Of course, this doesn't work. It never has and it never will. This style of confession makes an idol of our sins and shortcomings. The focus is on the sin itself, and not the Father's nature. There is nothing wrong with being specific in our confessions. Being as specific as we can is indeed best. But we don't have to understand all the ins and outs of all our failures, for how can we without the Spirit's help? It's impossible for us to line them up like fence posts across a Texas field. What we can do is bring what we know about ourselves and what we've done to the Light. That's enough for now.

Confession is not for God, it's for us.

We mustn't think of confession as just a summary of wrongs or sins. In fact, the first movement of the Lord's Prayer is the more important form of confession—it is a declaration of what is most true: the nature and authority of God. That is why we have creeds and psalms that are read and sung (confessed) in the company of others. There is a greater story, a more universal Truth that guides and shapes our confession. God is faithful in and to our struggle and will indeed finish the good work that he started.

Heaven knows the hardest thing for us to surrender is our opinion of ourselves. We think that no one, including God, could know what we're all about. But God's Spirit knows the truths and the lies that we've hidden from ourselves. The ones that are so attached to our sense of self that we can't remember a time when they weren't there. Confession cuts through these lies, offering an inward journey home.

God designed confession to be intimate and relational, a moment that builds trust and mutual revelation. Its power lies in its ability to gather three things that seem to be in conflict: the nature of God, who we are as a child of God, and our sins. Despite what you may've been told, the Father's not afraid of sin. In fact, he tells us to come boldly to the throne of grace that we might find help in our time of need.[2] The Father knows that when we need him the most is when sin fractures our lives. But in these same moments, the Accuser tries to either rationalize our sins or beat us into shame; both tactics are an attempt to block God's reconciling power.

When we bring our failures to the Father, we are, in a sense, making a statement: neither sin nor the Accuser gets to define us, only the Father can do that. His Word, not our sin, is the final authority.

As children of God, only the sins we retain hold power over us.

When we confess our sins, whether we confess directly to God or to a confidant, we are defying the sin, refusing to let it rule us in the shadows of accusation and deception.

Everyone knows that the best lies are served with some truth, and the Accuser leverages this fact better than anyone. When we've fallen short, he will peskily remind us that we missed the mark, but he doesn't stop there. He goes on to claim that because we missed it, we will always miss it, suggesting that we hide ourselves from the Father of lights.

So how do we combat the Father of Lies? How do we emerge from the shadows and step into the Light?

The most powerful thing you can do to disarm the Accuser is agree with the truth in his lie. Admitting that you have done wrong is not bad, but taking on shame only perpetuates sin. Guilt is tied to what you've done; shame is tied to who you are. Guilt says, "I missed it." Shame says, "I will always miss it, because that's just who I am."

So many of us struggle not to listen to the Accuser because we know that, in a way, the Accuser speaks truth. That is why we need to bring what we've done to the Father, so he, through the work of the Spirit, can help separate what we've done from who we are. Confession is where the lie that is not all a lie bows a knee to the Truth that is all Truth.

We confess our sins (to God and each other) that we may be healed, for disease is nothing less than disintegration and disharmony. There is a healing power in the prayer of confession that makes us whole. The breastplate of righteousness and shield of faith Paul wrote about in Ephesians 6 block the Accuser's lies, but sometimes we forget to put on our weaponry. We mustn't forget, though, that our strength is our righteousness in Christ, which is found in the Son's covenant faithfulness; we are in Christ and coheirs of the promise. This is our confidence. And when we pray from this place of assurance, our prayers are powerful and will do their work.[3]

In Mark 1 there's a beautiful moment between Jesus and a leper (it's also captured in Matt. 8). In the Jewish world, leprosy was associated with filth and sin. It was a virulent skin disease, and if someone contracted it, they were likely of the sordid sort and unfit for society. Lepers were cast out and forced to live among themselves, separated from the greater community.

And they were not allowed to hide their leprosy. Instead, they were supposed to wear torn clothes, cover their mouth and nose, and yell "unclean" anytime they were in the company of others. Certainly, no one was supposed to touch them.

But the leper in Mark's first chapter is bold and apparently one of those people who folks mistake as a rule-breaker because they live by a higher and better set of rules—rules that Scripture calls "the law of Christ" or "law of liberty."[4]

Jesus reaches out and touches the leper, undermining the notion that God cannot reach us in our sin. It is true that God cannot look on sin *favorably*. But contrary to what religion boasts, he will never let sin set the terms of engagement, and Jesus made it clear that God will certainly enter the mess of our sins.

We should keep in mind that Jesus didn't have to touch the man, nor was he supposed to. Scripture records many miracles that didn't require Jesus to touch people. But there's something here that we shouldn't miss: Jesus *wanted* to touch the man. He wanted to restore his humanity. Only God knows how long it had been since this man had felt the touch of another. The leper needed a healing touch, and Jesus never denied a request for healing.

But when it comes to healing, Jesus could help only those who knew they were sick and believed he could do something about their brokenness. Search the Gospels, and you will not find an account where Jesus heals someone without them participating through faith (or the faith of friends). Everyone who was healed by Jesus believed there was healing on the other side of their surrender to his touch. The exact result may've been murky, but they knew there was something better or *other* beyond their condition.

Let's not forget that there were many people, lepers included, who withdrew from Jesus and didn't invite his touch. What this tells us is that the only ones who were (and are) in danger of not participating in Jesus's life are those who don't surrender their sin and brokenness to him.

As much as we'd like to avoid the topic, we cannot deny sin's effect on us. Sin separates and sunders, fragments and frustrates, divides and degrades. It is a violation of relationship, first with God, then ourselves and others. We can talk about sin in a metaphysical sense, with theories of atonement and such, but sin is tangible and material. Go cheat on your spouse, lie to your boss, gossip about your friends, and see what happens. Sin is a real problem that affects real people. That's why God took on real flesh to deal with it.

As Saints, we don't have to be slaves to sin and its power. This doesn't mean that we won't sin. It means that we have a choice if we sin. We can surrender sin to God and allow him to do what only he can do: redeem it. Or we can hold on to sin, excusing and justifying it, allowing its shame to keep us from running to the Father.

Scripture makes it clear that we can know complete freedom from sin's authority. As Romans 8 tells us, "There is therefore now no condemnation. . . . For the law of the Spirit of life has set [us] free in Christ Jesus from the law of sin and death."[5] This does not, however, mean that our lives won't be affected by sin's pains. We live in a disintegrated world that is full of broken and hurting people who break and hurt people. But we are strengthened for patient and supernatural service in knowing and believing that sin and condemnation are not the final authority.

By God's grace, we can overcome sin in ways we never knew were possible. While grace takes us higher than we ever thought we could go, it also stoops lower than we ever imagined it could.

It gets in the dirt and liberates the condemned. It is patient and steadfast, even when we are inconsistent and faithless. But grace cannot and will not endorse sin as what's best for our flourishing.

For now, we must live in the tension of preaching good news that takes the problem of sin seriously. We must, as Jesus did, reject moralism and embrace godly morality.

Moralism is what happens when we forget the purpose of morality. Let's not forget that Jesus did condemn the Pharisees' affinity for moralism, which was evident in how they prioritized the tithing of spices over people.[6]

That being said, one of the most important functions of prayer is to develop a God-conscious morality. True morality is the proper interplay of relationships. It is dynamic yet constant. In Scripture, it's called the "law of Christ" and "royal law," among other names.

What we do and how we live isn't just a personal matter; it's a kingdom matter because our actions affect real people. The Father's desire is to cultivate our conscience, granting us kingdom consciousness, so we can know and see this to be true. But biblical morality stripped from its relational context degenerates into religious pride, or moralism, something we're all too familiar with.

————————

Paul made the claim that the Holy Spirit spoke through his conscience—that the two worked together to direct his words and efforts.

> I am speaking the truth in Christ—I am not lying; my conscience bears me witness in the Holy Spirit. (Rom. 9:1)

Our conscience is a way the Voice speaks to us and directs our lives. It is an inner witness or God-awareness that leads us forward. But based on what we find in Scripture, the conscience is like a communication line that can be hijacked and repurposed by the Accuser.

When we look at the Greek word for *conscience*, we discover that it's tied to awareness or consciousness. But this consciousness, evidently, can be corrupted. We need to wake up to the mind of Christ, which is both eternal and universal.

Paul writes,

> Knowing the fear of the Lord, we persuade others. But what we are is known to God, and I hope it is known also to your conscience. (2 Cor. 5:11)

Notice that, for Paul, knowing is tied to the fear of the Lord. In other words, we come to know the truth of all things as we believe that only God knows the truth of all things. How's that for a paradox?

A conscience is trustworthy when it is God-conscious.

Movements and religions attempt to manipulate the conscience, bullying people into compliance. They do this by telling us that we're not the right sort of people if we don't conform to their desires or agenda. In these moments of pressure, a pure or surrendered conscience will be a conduit for the Voice, and we will know what to do in times of duress.[7]

Humans were created in God's nature and therefore possess a desire for good. But the Accuser has a way of manipulating our inherent desire to do what is right, convincing us that good is bad and bad is good. We see this played out in the narrative about the tree of the knowledge of good and evil. *Did God really say that?*

If sin is indeed "missing the mark," then one of the best ways to make sure someone misses the mark is to point them at the wrong target. That's exactly what the Accuser did to Adam and Eve and continues to do to us today: he corrupts the conscience by pointing it toward the wrong mark. Let's look at two practical ways the Accuser does this and what the corrupted conscience, in these two forms, looks like.

The first thing a corrupted conscience will do is drive us away from the person, presence, and power of God. The compromised conscience becomes a weapon of shame, and the soul becomes isolated, hopeless, and confused. Unfortunately, religion has often leveraged this corruption of conscience to modify people's behavior, making people believe that they are always "in trouble." Such manipulation is powerful and effective because we are, in a sense, in trouble when left to ourselves. The wages of sin is death, after all. But we don't have to get our stuff right before we go to the Father. In fact, the only way we get our stuff right is by going to the Father. Bringing our failure and dissonance to God clarifies conscience, helping us live in a way that honors God's design for human flourishing. And this invitation is not singular or conditional; it is always there for us.

Jesus gave his life to make it clear that nothing, not even humanity's killing of his Son, could separate us from the Father's love. That is why the writer of Hebrews penned these words:

How much more will the blood of Christ, who through the eternal Spirit offered himself without blemish to God, purify our conscience from dead works to serve the living God. (9:14)

Let us draw near with a true heart in full assurance of faith, with our hearts sprinkled clean from an evil conscience and our bodies washed with pure water. (10:22)

It is only by knowing that we are safe with the Father, reconciled to him by the Son and Spirit, that we can bring our dissonance to him and have our conscience purified. God is the Consuming Fire, the One whose flames heal though they burn. There are things in us that are not us. They pretend to be authentic or true, but they are nothing more than the effects of sin and brokenness, stretched out across generations and time. What is truly *us* is never lost in surrender.

The second thing a corrupted conscience will do is deny the existence of a universal right and wrong that proceeds from God and belongs to him. C. S. Lewis used the term *Law of Human Nature* to describe a universal conscience or inward voice that resonates with God's design for human flourishing. He argued that across the great civilizations, there may be differences between their concepts of morality, but these differences have never amounted to a total difference. He then provides examples of what is commonly held to be good across societies and suggests that it would be preposterous and injurious for society to trade what it consciously knows to be mutually beneficial and good for what is clearly wrong (or evil). To sum up his argument he asks us, the reader, to imagine the lunacy of a world where one claims that two plus two equals five.[8]

———

Our world has been shaped by postmodernism, which denies the existence of absolute Truth—a claim that is, in and of itself, a contradiction. With nothing to stand on, postmodernism crumbles under its own weight and has been, largely, replaced with a post-postmodern movement that wants to rewrite Truth. This "new" paradigm of Truth is, for the most part, hostile to what was previously considered true and does not share the "anything goes" postmodern spirit. Rather, it seeks to conform every point of human interaction to its purposes and design. This movement has hijacked "conscience," reducing it from something that is God-aware to something that is man- or agenda-manipulated. Championing a pseudo acceptance, a shadow of the acceptance that they likely "missed" in the Father, these souls often refuse to accept anyone who doesn't align with their position, a position that looks an awful lot like religion at its worst.

These are dangerous times and there is much at stake. We need a God-oriented conscience to navigate the nuances and shades of brokenness around us. We need the wholeness of holiness, a wholeness that comes only with patience, a patience that is wrought in prayer. A patience that is strengthened in us as we repent and confess, bringing our sins and shortsightedness to the Father.

Confession is where the miracle of forgiveness becomes ever more personal and meaningful.

But when we deny that we both need forgiveness and are already forgiven, we become incapable of forgiving others. The cancel culture of our day is a direct result of people not receiving the Father's forgiveness. To know that we are forgiven, a forgiveness that is both gracious and necessary, is to navigate the differences and failures of our world with humility, patience, and understanding. The Father is patient with us, and he expects us to be patient with others. It'd be good for us to keep in mind that patience and steadfastness are the first and last attributes of love in 1 Corinthians 13. "Love is patient. . . . [Love] never ends."[9]

Do we know that we are safe with God? Safe enough to confess? Asher shares his failures with me because he knows that I see more in him than he sees in himself. He knows that I will stand with him no matter what. I regularly ask him: "Asher, why do I love you? . . . Is it because you're a hard worker? Smart? Kind? Funny?"

"No, Dad, you love those things about me, but that's not why you love me . . . you love me because I'm your son."

I've seen the effect this certainty has had on my kids. They trust me with moments, failures, and fears that lead to deep connection and trust. Nothing is off-limits, and they know that.

We should know it too.

11

Me to We

All the ends of the earth shall remember
    and turn to the LORD,
and all the families of the nations
    shall worship before you.
For kingship belongs to the LORD,
    and he rules over the nations.

Psalm 22:27–28

The one who was most alienated, condemned, and forsaken . . .
became the fountain head of reconciliation and so frees and
unites humanity.

Kosuke Koyama, *Three Mile an Hour God*

When we talk with God, we do so in the company
of others.

In Matthew 6, Jesus does tell us to pray in our
room with the door shut, but he also instructs us to open our

hearts by praying "Our Father." The kingdom of God advances at the intersection of relationship, so the Father designed prayer to bring us together, helping us see the world as more than the sum of our individual cares and concerns. It is only within the awareness of this greater world that we find the perspective to make sense of and navigate our own lives.

In matters of prayer, Jesus prefers the pronouns *our*, *we*, and *us* over *me*, *myself*, and *I*. The Lord's Prayer flies in the face of individualism, and it belongs to a kingdom that confounds the tribalism of our age. The Prayer's very nature beckons us to be grasped by something higher and better than the false dualities of our day.

The challenge is, most of us grew up at the table of an individualistic gospel. The theme of God's plan to reconcile nations and peoples got smooshed between a myopic view of heaven and hell, and in its place we were offered a formulaic prayer that makes sure you, as an individual, end up in the right place. Holiness lost its communal form and was reduced to personal moralism and procedure.

Common practice is now to limit holiness to following rules or not sinning, and it's done by us alone. But Scripture portrays God's holiness as something that redefines our small ideas of harmony, integrity, and beauty. We struggle with the terms *holy*, *holiness*, and *holy ones* because, in their true form, they're terribly difficult to contain. They convey an *otherness* that belongs to God. It's a quality that transcends all other qualities and is not to be confined or belittled. Holiness is the innermost or superlative attribute of a being. It is how we must relate to and understand each other. When it comes to the other, there is always something "more" that mustn't become a slave to reductionism.[1]

The creatures in God's throne room cry "Holy!" not because it makes a nice melody when you string three of them together but because with each moment a new facet of God's nature is revealed to them. "Holy!" is not a lyric; it's a shout.

We cultivate the fear of the Lord in prayer as we refuse to make God (and others) submit to our kingdoms. We cannot make God the god of our political, cultural, ethnic, national, or societal preferences and designs. To fear God is the beginning of the only wisdom that transcends dissonance, and true knowledge of God's nature is the only place where we find the understanding we need to navigate this cultural moment. Through prayer we are filled with grace to reconcile the irreconcilable, finding a beloved assurance that there is another dimension of belonging, and its pathway is not tolerant indifference but a holy love that unfolds in righteousness, peace, joy, and patience.

"I cannot work out God's will in my own life," wrote Thomas Merton, "unless I also consciously help other men to work out His will in theirs. His will, then, is our sanctification, our transformation in Christ, our deeper and fuller integration with other men. And this integration results not in the absorption or disappearance of our own personality, but in its affirmation and its perfection."[2]

God's kingdom represents distinct nations, backgrounds, ethnicities, and socioeconomics, and he likes it that way. The prophetic vision of the age to come is marked by tribes, peoples, tongues, and nations. God is not trying to make us all the same. The diversity showcases his creativity. There is a dignity in difference. But beyond our individual or cultural stories, there is The Story, the one that we're all part of. And in this story, we are members of the universal family of God, and when we come together as *one* family, we begin to reveal the collective glory that belongs to our God. Whoever said, "It takes a whole world to reveal a whole Christ" might be on to something.

True prayer is wandering into the worthiness of it all. It's being grasped by God's holy nature and what God's holiness invites us into, here and now, among his creation. Such prayer is the strength of our worship, a worship that is more than a slow song, for it is the integration of our lives with the plans, peoples, and purposes of God. It is holy work, a living sacrifice. A willingness to go wherever and to whomever the Father sends us.

There's this story about a man and a fish. I'm sure you've heard it before.

It's one of those wild stories in the Bible. The kind of story that challenges scholars and scientists alike, provoking them to label its plotline as a parody. We tend to get caught up in the whole fish bit—or was it a whale?—but this story isn't really about a fish. It seems to me the fish has largely become a distraction, hiding the real reason why the narrative has a place in the pages of Scripture. This is a sinister story. One that exposes the darkest side of our humanity, the reason why Jesus told his first-century companions that "an evil and adulterous generation seeks for a sign, but no sign will be given to it except the sign of the prophet Jonah."[3]

Jonah's story, whether we like it or not, is our story.

The story begins with Jonah receiving a word from the Lord. YHWH, the God of Israel, tells his prophet to go to Nineveh, the great city of the Assyrians, sworn enemies of God's people. God's reason for sending Jonah?

Call out against it, for their evil has come before me. (Jon. 1:2)

But Jonah doesn't obey.

The Ninevites are his sworn enemies, oppressors of God's chosen people. So Jonah flees from God to find a ship that can take him in the opposite direction, to a place called Tarshish. Once aboard the ship, Jonah settles into a nice place below deck to take a nap. I guess somehow Jonah convinced himself that he escaped the presence of the Lord—an assumption the text mentions multiple times—and can now rest in peace, free from the irrational demands of his God, a God whose presence is, based on Jonah's actions, limited to a geographic location and whose interest shouldn't extend beyond a specific group of people.

But not long after Jonah "escapes" God's presence, the wind and sea revolt against Jonah's slumber, making a mess of his plan. At this point in the story, the crew has done everything practical to save their skins and have now turned to calling on any god who can save them from Poseidon's grip. When calling out to gods doesn't work, the crew figures that maybe one of their own caused the tempest and resort to casting lots in hopes of identifying the guilty person.

The idea of the crew casting lots while the ship is being tossed and turned seems comical to me. I imagine them tearing apart the already doomed ship to find a bag of lots that was tossed from its normal place and found a new home in a nook or cranny. After the bag is finally recovered, maybe the crew had to quickly locate a decently flat place to discern the portents. When my family plays any dice game, we have a rule that the dice must be rolled into a box and the box must sit squarely on the table. The stationary box keeps the dice from being manipulated by the slight lean of a hand. So, when I think of these men casting lots, I think of a high-risk game that would, of course, require a fair playing field. After all, the loser could become fish food.

The lot falls on Jonah, begging the crew to ask, "Who are you and what have you done?!" Jonah responds with no small measure of pretension, boasting of his nationality and the superiority of his God, the "God . . . who made the sea and the dry land,"[4] a fact that must have slipped his mind a few verses earlier when he ran from his mighty God's presence.

Jonah then tells them to cast him into the sea, which the men eventually do with not a small degree of reluctance. Jonah is saved by the fish and the pagan crew worships Jonah's God, offering sacrifices and vows to YHWH.

We should wonder why Jonah didn't tell the crew to take him back to Joppa or even in the direction of Nineveh. Wouldn't that act of obedience calm the tempest? I would argue that Jonah's request to be thrown into the ocean was an act of defiance. Jonah is essentially telling God, "I'd rather die in the ocean than go to Nineveh!" What is this man's deal? Why is he so opposed to going to Nineveh? Clearly, it's not because Jonah is afraid to lose his life. This is the guy, after all, who sleeps during a tempest and then casually tells the crew to sacrifice him to the sea.

There's something else at play here.

After three days and nights of pouting and feeling sorry for himself, Jonah finally relents and offers a religious, half-hearted prayer of repentance. YHWH tells the fish to vomit Jonah onto land and then, for the second time,[5] instructs Jonah to head to Nineveh.

Jonah obeys.

Scripture tells us that "Nineveh was an exceedingly great city, three days' journey in breadth,"[6] but Jonah decides to travel only a single day's worth into the city. And his message held no promise, hope, or even an invitation for them to repent. He, in a sense, just told them they were doomed and would be destroyed in forty days, a number that is not mentioned before this point in the story. If we're generous, we could say that Jonah completed half of the assignment, yet God uses his half-hearted obedience to deliver a message to the king, and the king delivers the message that should've been on Jonah's lips. The king calls the nation to repentance and mourning, and God hears their cries and spares the city.

But God's mercy "displeased Jonah exceedingly."[7]

It is at this point that we're finally given a clear look into Jonah's psyche. We now know why this Hebrew prophet was so bent on avoiding Nineveh. There is no need for conjecture or guesswork, for Jonah is unmade by the distress and reveals to us, the readers, what both God and Jonah have known all along: "O LORD, is not this what I said when I was yet in *my country*? That is why I made haste to flee to Tarshish; for I knew that you are a gracious God and merciful, slow to anger and abounding in steadfast love, and relenting from disaster."[8]

Jonah is a nationalist. The idea of *his* God extending mercy to the enemy was too much for him. Rather than embrace this strange demonstration of God's goodness, he complains that YHWH is extending mercy, love, and compassion to the alien and outsider. This benevolence is too much for him. The Assyrians were his enemy and oppressor, and Jonah was a protector of Israel; he was the prophet known for galvanizing Israel to restore its boundaries and keep infidels outside its borders, where they belong.[9] All of this just felt so unfair!

So what does Jonah do? He putters, pouts, and eventually asks God to kill him. Chasing some form of consolation, he sets up camp just outside the city, hoping that God would regain his sanity and slaughter the Assyrians. Amid Jonah's brooding, God causes a plant to miraculously grow and extend its shade over Jonah's head. This simple act of kindness causes Jonah, the man who was just asking God to kill him, to become exceedingly glad. He curls up in his little booth and enjoys a night of peace. *Surely, this is a good omen that God is on my side and against the Ninevites*, he reasons.

Jonah, like so many of us, knows how to think only dualistically: us versus them. Win or lose. Black or white. Chosen or rejected. Slave or free. Secular or sacred. But for Jonah, distress comes with the dawn. The confirmation of his election, the blessed covering of his calling, has withered and died. He now finds himself, once again, to be merely the outsider on a hill, whining and complaining that God is transforming his enemies into his brothers and sisters.

Jonah is furious: his exact words are, "I do well to be angry, angry enough to die."[10] Any demonstration of divine mercy that wasn't directed toward him and his people was an affront to Jonah's religiosity. Like the Pharisees, Jonah used orthodoxy to bolster a sense of elitism, rejecting the idea that God could have sheep of a different fold.[11] Jonah conveniently forgot that God originally called Israel to be a priest for the nations: a task that Israel failed to understand and pursue, leading to violence, elitism, and oppression among Israel and the nations it was called to serve. Back in Genesis 12, God promised that through Abraham's family, Israel, all the families of the earth would be blessed. Unfortunately, what had begun as a priestly blessing for the nations turned into nationalism and idolatry.

The book of Jonah ends with God's very words, giving us a window into the beautifully robust character of God.

And should not I pity Nineveh, that great city, in which there are more than 120,000 persons who do not know their right hand from their left, and also much cattle? (4:11)

I chuckle when I read the bit at the end, "also much cattle." You animal lovers should get a kick out of that.

This is a story about us.

————————

Religion tends to work out a way to encourage or tolerate hostility toward the outsider, the heathen, the marginalized. The disdain is often considered righteous and justified.

Yet on the Cross, Jesus took on all our hostility; his flesh bore the marks of our political (Rome) and religious (Jewish leaders) hate. The Cross epitomizes humanity at its best even though it is the result of humanity at its worst. Every flow of human separation reconverged and was judged in Jesus's sacrifice.

It takes great strength for us to believe that this is true.

It's easier to believe that the splits among us are final, that our proclivity toward sin will overpower God's power to redeem and reconcile. We cannot make peace on our own, but Christ is our peace, and his Spirit unifies our hearts in what Paul calls the "bond of peace."[12] The Integrator will win the day when the lie that is not all a lie is displaced by the Truth that is all true. But we don't have to just sit on our hands and wait for that day; even now God has sent his Spirit as a guarantee of the age to come, the age when humankind will trade weapons for worship, sin for salvation, hate for love.

In the name of the Beloved, the name that is above every name, all things are united in life, things in both heaven and earth. In his flesh, the dividing wall of hostility is broken down, and we are reconciled to God.[13] Religiosity tells us that we must overcome sin on our own and reconcile God to ourselves, but the Bible tells us a different story. Nowhere in Scripture are we told that we must reconcile God to us; God does the reconciling, the wooing, the calling. He has never stopped. We've just forgotten how to listen.

The Voice speaks.

When the Garden reality ended, God still met with his people. But we turned to our own devices, wanting to build kingdoms of our own. Violence became the currency of strength. And as we moved away from God, violence took on a religious form, a cathartic exercise that transferred our brokenness and lack onto an animal or person.

We continue to scapegoat to this day, blaming a political party, race, gender, nation, society, or sexual orientation for our problems. But external dissonance is nothing more than what happens when we deny the dissonance within. We need a scapegoat, so we locate those who are *other* than us, the ones with a different form of brokenness, a brokenness that we can blame for our pain. If they would just be [fill in the blank] or do [fill in the blank] then this world would be right in a month.

––––––––––

There is a mystery to human flourishing that we, evidently, still can't grasp. According to Paul, it is *the* mystery of the gospel, which has now been revealed to the Saints.[14] In other words, it's what the gospel and kingdom are all about.

This mystery is that the Gentiles are fellow heirs, members of the same body, and partakers of the promise in Christ Jesus through the gospel. (Eph. 3:6)

Paul goes on to say that "there is one body and one Spirit—just as you were called to the one hope that belongs to your call—one Lord, one faith, one baptism, one God and Father of all, who is over all and through all and in all."[15] This cosmic unity surpasses knowledge, leaving us in holy wonder. Or as Paul puts it, "For this reason I bow my knees before the Father, from whom every family in heaven and on earth is named."[16] The only reasonable response is to bow a knee because this Truth is far greater than anything we could've worked out on our own.

The gentile, the person who is an "outsider," belongs. They have always belonged, but we couldn't understand it. We see their presence in Jesus's lineage. Rahab of Jericho and Ruth of Moab remind us of God's promise to Abraham, that all the nations would be blessed through his family.

The mystery that has been hidden for ages and generations, a mystery hiding in plain sight, is that in Christ, God is reconciling the world—as in all peoples—to himself, not counting their sins against them.[17] We no longer have to scapegoat and blame. There's no need to vilify and judge. Jesus shed the blood of violence and broke down, in his flesh, the dividing wall. This is why the heavenly creatures and elders sing,

> Worthy are you to take the scroll
>   and to open its seals,
> for you were slain, and by your blood you ransomed
>   people for God
>   from every tribe and language and people and nation,
> and you have made them a kingdom and priests to our
>   God,
>   and they shall reign on the earth. (Rev. 5:9–10)

His death is the life of nations. Only in his death and life are we set free from the separating power of sin and can now resume our place as priests to God and stewards of his good world.

―――――――

After his resurrection, Jesus spent forty days with his followers, preparing them for what was to come. Scripture doesn't tell us much about this time, but we do know that Jesus spoke on the kingdom and the Spirit.[18]

Upon hearing all this talk about the kingdom, the disciples asked him, "Lord, will you at this time restore the kingdom to Israel?"[19] But Jesus didn't give them the answer they sought. Instead, he told them, "You will receive power when the Holy Spirit has come upon you." And then he reframes, once again, their perception of kingdom by adding, "And you will be my witnesses in Jerusalem and in all Judea and Samaria, and to the end of the earth."[20] In other words, the good news of the kingdom must extend beyond their home or comfort zone (Jerusalem and Judea) and reach the outcast and outsider (Samaria and the end of the earth). That was a hard message for them to swallow. The kingdom was supposed to look different. None of them expected Jesus to establish his kingdom by reconciling their enemies to God.

But Jesus had overcome the grave, so they decided to listen to him and wait in Jerusalem until the promise of the Father, God's Spirit, visited them. When the day of Pentecost arrived, they were filled with the Spirit and began to declare the Good News in other tongues. The Spirit empowered them to transcend cultural and linguistic barriers, and the disciples became, as it were, witnesses to the nations.

The fact that this happened on Pentecost was no accident. Pentecost (or *Shavuot*) marked the wheat harvest in Israel.[21] The Spirit was now empowering them to see that the fields of wheat, the nations, were ripe for the harvest, a truth that Jesus shared with them in John 4, after he invited a Samaritan woman to participate in the Good News. Many Orthodox rabbinic traditions teach that *Shavuot* commemorates the revelation of the Torah at Mount Sinai. In Acts 2, on that Pentecost, the law was reborn within God's original intent.

The nation of Israel was named and called out for service. They were to be a nation of priests for the nations. But they rejected this assignment at Sinai and demanded religion, something that looked like what they had known in Egypt (the reason they soon created a golden calf to be the object of their worship). God has always stooped within our religion to elevate us into higher forms of covenantal relationship, and we see this at Sinai, just as we would later see it in God's response to Israel's demand for a king. But instead of Israel serving the nations in the pattern of Christ, they exploited their favor, becoming a terror to both themselves and the nations they were called to serve.

It would take a book much bigger than this one to work through Sinai's implications and how they continue to impact our idea of God, worship, prayer, and others today. We forsook mystery at Sinai, demanding a religious system in its place. "We'll just do whatever you tell us to do, Moses!" But this has never been about "doing whatever God tells us to do." It's been about returning to Garden form, choosing to yield every bit of ourselves to the hope of the nations.

At Pentecost, by the Spirit, these Israelites who were not of the priestly tribe could embrace Israel's responsibility to be priests. And by saying yes to Jesus and the work of the Spirit, our lives also become the Good News to the nations. Paul describes it this way: "And you show that you are a letter from Christ delivered by us, written not with ink but with the Spirit of the living God, not on tablets of stone but on tablets of human hearts."[22]

It's easy to get concerned about what's happening on a global scale. These are dangerous times, marked by wars and rumors of war, political corruption and greed, darkness and despair. But what is our reasonable response? How do we pray when we're in the dark, so to speak?

We should note that Jesus's first imperative on prayer is that we should love our enemies and pray for those who persecute us,[23] for that is the pathway of our perfection; it's how we share in our Father's holiness. It's the only way we can pray and live in the reality of "Our Father." When we forsake the truth of God's otherness and what it means for us, we become slaves to the people we are called to serve. Biblically speaking, the people of God don't go into exile because of the wickedness that surrounds them; they go into exile when they participate in what unmakes the nations.

The cosmic fracturing that pits man against man is caused by the Accuser and his legion of dark powers. Paul tells us that "we do not wrestle against flesh and blood, but against the rulers, against the authorities, against the cosmic powers over this present darkness, against the spiritual forces of evil in the heavenly places."[24] We combat these forces by "praying at all times in the Spirit."[25] By listening to the Voice.

The demonic powers seek to divide and perpetuate the lie of disintegration. There are demonic splits in the souls of people that produce insanity and cellular destruction. Until one knows internal shalom (integration), they will intentionally or unintentionally contribute to the disintegration and chaos of our day.

If we make flesh and blood our enemy, we are fighting the wrong battle. We should instead be interceding on our brothers' and sisters' behalf, for as Jesus showed us, that is the best way to win over a nation.

The impersonal (and sometimes personal) vitriol that flies across social media isn't helping anyone. It leads to inadequate and unthoughtful responses that are polarized and polarizing. The enemy has a way of introducing lies in pairs. Then he makes the popcorn, sits back in a comfortable chair, and gets a good laugh at us arguing over which lie is better. A truth that is all too apparent in identity politics.

So before we launch an attack on someone (or something), why not spend five minutes genuinely praying for that person or situation first? I mean, really search out the Father's heart for them. I promise you, you'll feel better about your private conversations, and you'll probably post a lot less. Before we campaign for peace and equity, why not practice, learn, and extend such things within our home, church, school, or neighborhood? The *other* isn't just across the world. She's your snarky older sister. Your annoying coworker. Your hurting father.

At the end of her 1979 Nobel Prize acceptance speech, Mother Teresa famously said, "My prayer for you is that truth will bring prayer in our homes, and the fruit of prayer will be that we . . . will try to do something. First in our own home, our next door neighbor, in the country we live, in the whole world. And let us all join in that one prayer."[26]

Notice that for Mother Teresa, prayer is what's missing. Only when prayer enters our homes will we know what to do and why to do it. And this knowing begins with our own home and then extends into the greater world. Prayer always leads to action because it is active. The action will feel less like doing, though, and more like getting in on something that is already happening.

People who prayerfully search the heart of God for a moment know what to do in that moment. They speak with a gentle clarity, refusing to be dragged along by the rhetoric of the day. They understand that it is a person's reaction to a thing that determines what power it has over them. And when the time to act comes, they act with courage, relying on the Spirit's strength.

Howard Thurman, a civil rights leader who inspired Martin Luther King Jr., once penned these words:

> The forces at work in the world which seem to determine the future and the fate of mankind seem so vast, impersonal, and unresponsive to the will and desire of any individual that it is easy to abandon all hope for a sane and peaceful order to life for mankind. Nevertheless, it is urgent to hold steadily in mind the utter responsibility of the solitary individual to do everything with all his heart and mind to arrest the development of the consequence of private and personal evil resulting from the interaction of the impersonal forces that surround us. To cancel out between you and another all personal and private evil, to put your life squarely on the side of the good thing because it is good, and for no other reason, is to anticipate the kingdom of God at the level of your functioning.[27]

As a Black man living at the turn of the twentieth century, Dr. Thurman had every reason to embrace hopelessness and slide into an us versus them mentality. But he refused to get caught up in any activity that labeled and demeaned. For him, the fight against an impersonal evil must be won at the intersection of real persons. This is how we "anticipate the kingdom of God at the level of [our] functioning." Wow.

What would happen if we prayed and interceded for real people the way Jesus told us to? Our insults and condemnation won't deliver them from their sins. But when we, through prayer, awaken an awareness in our brother, he will attack his betrayal and disease as only he can—from the inside.[28] That's what we should pray for: awareness. For our sister to have eyes to see, ears to hear, a heart to perceive and understand. Even a glimmer of awareness can start a soul down the road of repentance, forgiveness, and reconciliation.

Forgiveness doesn't require a perfect understanding of fault. Forgiveness must only be offered. It is unconditional, but for it to have its intended effect, some level of awareness is a must. Forgiveness invites participation, a joint commitment to overcome the powers of estrangement, even when those powers hide in ambiguities and confused consciousness. That is why we need the Spirit to do the work that only the Integrator can do. Most people can't make heads or tails of their interior lives. And a soul that hasn't embraced the power of forgiveness is a danger to all.

And that is why we pray.

12

Forgiveness

Without forgiveness there is no future.

Desmond Tutu, *No Future
Without Forgiveness*

I can no longer condemn or hate a brother for whom I pray, no
matter how much trouble he causes me.

Dietrich Bonhoeffer, *Life Together*

Both Jesus and Stephen, the first martyr,[1] spent some of
their final breaths praying for their oppressors. To be
more specific, they asked God to forgive those who were
killing them . . . while they were being killed. Just sit with that
for a moment.

In Jesus's case, he pleaded for the Father to forgive his torturers because they didn't know what they did; their ignorance was
reason enough for their pardon. Of course, these guys knew

perfectly well how to kill people, and based on what we read in Scripture, they seemed to have turned killing into a sport with games and such. Yet still Jesus claimed that they didn't know what they did.

We look at Jesus and think, *Of course he could forgive the way he did. He's God.* But in Stephen we're confronted with a man like us. A man who waited tables and did odd jobs for widows. He was just one of the guys who found himself in the wrong place at the wrong time. Or maybe it was the right place at the right time?

Paul's life changed on the road to Damascus, but I believe his deliverance began at Stephen's death, the moment Stephen forgave Paul for killing him. One could say that Stephen spent his life for another, exhaling forgiveness with his final breath. Saul (Paul) approved Stephen's execution and then went on to pen nearly half of the books in the New Testament.

At his moment of death, Stephen did not cry out for a justice that was calculating or punitive. The man, "full of the Holy Spirit,"[2] was completely immersed in what is ultimately real, and from that place he could do nothing else but cry that his oppressor would be released from his oppression. This is creative justice. Kingdom justice.

Stephen couldn't have known what that day would bring. There had been persecution, sure, but no one had traded their life for the chance to share the Good News that was written on their hearts because of Jesus's life, death, and resurrection. But this waiter wielded rhetoric that could not be refuted. He was full of grace, faith, and power, his inner life energized by the unshakable Truth that is wrought only in communion with Truth. Different groups of religious experts entered the scene to put this table-waiting man in his place. "But they could not withstand the wisdom and the Spirit with which [Stephen] was speaking."[3]

These religious leaders grasped for what was most sacred to them: their temple and their law. For them, these sacred constructs represented their power and promise. A way for them to insulate themselves from the dangerous gentile world. But Stephen was aware of a greater story: the one that God promised to Abraham. And that is why Stephen begins his story with Abraham, and not Moses. Toward the end of his plea, our martyr quotes Isaiah:

> Heaven is my throne,
>   and the earth is my footstool.
> What kind of house will you build for me,
>   says the Lord,
>   or what is the place of my rest?
> Did not my hand make all these things? (Acts 7:49–
>   50; see also Isa. 66:1–2)

Stephen then tells them that they resist the Spirit's work, the work of reconciling the nations to the Father's heart, of preaching repentance and acceptance to all peoples. It's a message that the prophets knew and understood; some of them even died for it. In a curious way, the prophets would speak of the nations being judged yet somehow saved through judgment. These things don't make sense to the learned; such words confound the wise. But they are true and the substance of a truth that we can build our lives on.

Stephen had opened the conversation. He could hear the Voice. Seeing things clearly, he knew that the gospel subverts religiosity and exclusivity. His were dangerous words. Gods and religions are better kept in temples and ritual. When the holy moves into hearts and homes, souls are delivered from the splitting power of sin. One day his words would be carried by Paul, the forgiven and reformed Pharisee who would spend most of his life reconciling the outsider. A life empowered by some of Stephen's final breaths . . .

Lord, don't hold this sin against him.

————————

We love the story of the paralytic man, the one with the best friends ever. Friends who broke a roof, most likely Jesus's own roof,[4] so that he could be made whole. But the story is about more than a broken roof. There are assumptions about God, sin, and forgiveness that must be broken as well.

When Jesus saw their faith, he declared, "Son, your sins are forgiven."[5] We should notice that "their faith" led to the forgiveness of the man's sins. This, of course, flies in the face of our individualist view of sin and forgiveness. We'd prefer the text to read, "When Jesus saw the man's faith." But it doesn't, and there's a reason for that.

Forgiveness and sin are communal matters. "Forgive us our sins, for we ourselves forgive everyone who is indebted to us."[6] We don't live in a vacuum of our decisions. Our lives intersect with others in every possible way. Forgiveness is the central theme of the gospel because it's the path of reconciliation to God, to ourselves, and to others. It's miraculous because it overcomes the disintegrating power of sin and releases the healing power of the Spirit.

"Forgiveness," writes N. T. Wright, "is more like the air in your lungs. There's only room for you to inhale the next lungful when you've just breathed out the previous one. If you insist on withholding it, the kiss of life that you may desperately need, you won't be able to take any more in yourself, and you will suffocate very quickly."[7]

Spend time with anyone (including yourself) who is suffocating from offense or unforgiveness, and you'll know Wright's words to be true. These people are offended with their neighbor, the government, their city, their spouse, their coworkers . . . the list swelling until it consumes their whole world.

To forgive is to disrupt the flow of this world.

———

There's a moment after Jesus's resurrection when he shows up and shows off his scars. His message to the disciples was simple: peace. But not a peace like the world's, where the stronger or more "right" or more intelligent party bullies the weaker or offending party into submission. No. This is a different sort of peace. One that comes only with the breath of forgiveness.

Jesus's hands, feet, and side were reminders to those closest to him that they left him to die alone. Only the disciple who called himself the beloved was there when the scars were made. The others abandoned, betrayed, or denied him. They had reason to be afraid of the resurrected Jesus. This was, after all, the same Jesus who told them that if they denied him before men, he would deny them before his Father.[8]

But Jesus offered them peace, wholeness, shalom—and the proof was in his scars. He had fought a bloody battle with sin, brokenness, and death. And now he, the Prince of Peace, invited his followers to know peace with God and man, even while their failure was still fresh. "As the Father has sent me, even so I am sending you."[9]

Normally, scars—whether of mind, heart, or body—remind

us that the world is dangerous and that we should be on our guard. Each scar tells a story of abuse, abandonment, betrayal, disappointment. But Jesus's resurrected body proves that in the Eternal Now our scars can become sacred and holy, evidence of his power to heal, restore, and redeem.

To punctuate this moment, Jesus "breathed on them and said to them, 'Receive the Holy Spirit. If you forgive the sins of any, they are forgiven them; if you withhold forgiveness from any, it is withheld.'"[10] The Greek word translated "breathed" is found nowhere else in the New Testament, and in the Septuagint, which is the Greek Old Testament, it is found only in Genesis 2:7, when God breathed his life into humankind. This was a moment when Jesus invited them to join his new creation work, a work that would be breathed into the world as they breathed in the Spirit's integrating power.

The sobering part of all this, though, is that Jesus told them if they refused to forgive, they would somehow be blocking or holding back the Spirit. In other words, to refuse to forgive would be to deny the power of the Cross, reducing Jesus's scars to nothing more than broken flesh. These disciples missed it at times, but even they knew that withholding forgiveness wasn't really an option, a truth that their lives after this interaction made clear.

Jesus was putting the finishing touches on a lesson that was years in the making. Our world disintegrates through violence, hatred, and unforgiveness. There are real sins that fracture and frustrate our humanity, and only the power of ultimate forgiveness can set us free to see the brokenness for what it is; only then can we lead people back to the Father.

The fact that Jesus rose from the grave validated what he had always said about himself and his authority: Jesus is the reconciler of all things, and if he says a man's sins are forgiven, they are forgiven. If he tells a body to be whole, it is whole. If he tells a mountain to move, it moves. And he sends us with his authority to do this same work.

But we don't like to forgive. It feels like we're letting someone off the hook. Like the whole thing is just a big injustice. Some of us withhold forgiveness until we feel like the person gets what they deserve. Here's the problem with that, though. We're not capable of measuring out what a person deserves. Do we sit outside of time? Do we know what's in the heart of a person? Can we be in every place at once? Can we determine every cause and effect? Are we ever without bias or preference?

The sobering truth is that the person we condemn, we cease to understand. To condemn is to make a final judgment, to say that I've seen the end of the road for you, and it goes nowhere worth going. Only God, the One who has seen the end, can offer final judgments. Our part is to participate in God's ministry of reconciliation so we can grow in the truth about God, ourselves, and each other. It is only then that we can judge to reconcile.

Most of us judge from a place of pain or frustration or disappointment. We're vindictive, punitive, calculating in our judgment. *How dare they do that! They must make things right!* But these negative feelings are sustained by the illusion that our brother or sister *knows* and *benefits* from what they do to us. "The ability to do evil or be evil is not freedom but a sickness," wrote Anthony De Mello, "for it implies a lack of consciousness and sensitivity."[11] We may be broken and bruised by their evil, but their life is perpetually bound by sin's unmaking power.

When we see their behavior as a sickness that torments their soul, we can respond with clarity and compassion. It is only then that we can pray, "Father, forgive them, for they know not what they do."

To have compassion literally means *to suffer with*, so can we have compassion toward those whose pain does not in some way become our own?

A few weeks ago, I shared a dinner with a friend who was in town for a few days. We met at a restaurant that uses picnic tables to foster communal seating. It's a popular place and the tables are close together, leaving mere inches between them. About thirty minutes into our meal, a new group slid into the table behind me, bumping me several times in the process. I hardly thought anything of it, though, because with the tables being so close together, they didn't have the option not to bump me. But a few minutes later, I took a good jab to the side.

I grew up wrestling with brothers, so it didn't faze me too much. I figured one of the guys got excited telling a story and lost control of his elbow. So, I just kept talking with my friend. A few minutes later, though, I took another hit. *Okay*, I thought, *maybe this guy's a bit clumsy and lacks spatial awareness. If he does it again, I'll say something.* Sure enough, a couple minutes later, I took another hit. At this point, I was annoyed and ready to have some words with the guy, but I also wasn't trying to start a fight. I slowly turned around to survey the scene behind me. As soon as my head started to swivel, I noticed that a lady in her midforties was looking at me. It was like she was expecting my head to turn. Her eyes caught mine, and she mouthed an apology: "I'm so sorry, sir; he has autism."

Immediately, my frustration turned to compassion. It was a tight space, and the young man was triggered by the environment.

I also realized that he was likely having an adverse response to his mother's attempts to calm him down, for my sake, which led to him inadvertently hitting me more. The best thing for me to do was to assure the mother that I was used to being hit and could handle it, while, as best I could, sliding over on the bench to give her son as much elbow space as possible.

Thank God that I became aware before I acted. Without awareness, I would've done more harm to the boy's mom, the boy, and myself. Another point to make is that it would've been unhelpful for me to stay where I was. The boy needed some space. I needed to withdraw, if you will, for his sake (and my own). But my withdrawal was from a place of compassion and not anger or disgust. There are times when forgiveness requires us to withdraw from someone's presence, because by hurting us, they are hurting themselves. But even the withdrawal should be an act of compassion.

When we accept the truth that our brother or sister, like the young man with autism, is suffering and doesn't know what they do, we are forced to bring our pain and confusion to the Father in prayer. In this place of compassionate surrender, the Spirit gives us eyes to see what part we play in their liberation.

The kingdom of God advances at the intersection of relationship, the reason forgiveness must be the central pathway of human formation.

But our world seeks to establish peace without the difficult work of forgiveness. Such efforts toward reconciliation or integration fall apart because they aren't built on the foundation of God's forgiveness and our need to be forgiven. Rome championed peace, the Pax Romana, but no peace can last without a communal commitment that is energized by the daily prayer and practice of forgiveness.

Please understand that I am not suggesting we just overlook sin. To forgive is to stare down a sin until you see it within the truth of ultimate reality. Only then can you hear the Voice and know how to respond. Let's not forget that Paul instructed the Corinthians to cast out the sexually immoral man and "hand [him] over to Satan for the destruction of the flesh."[12] But this judgment was rendered from a place of loving awareness, for Paul went on to write "that his spirit may be saved on the day of the Lord." Most scholars believe that in a later letter, Paul told the Corinthians to restore the man. How could Paul, from afar, understand the nuances of such a difficult situation? Prayer.

Those whose prayers aren't energized by a revelation of the Father's nature and the promise of his kingdom struggle to forgive. For them, life is just a big ledger, and they are always in the red, and since they're prisoners of the red, surely others must be as well. So, they enforce red awareness, making sure each of us knows our place. And when we can't pay our debts, we are cancelled, rejected, dehumanized, and condemned forever—or at least until we can pay what we owe. But how can any of us truly know what we owe? How can we measure the effects of our sins? The disintegrating effect of sin is not singular or small. Scripture talks of it in terms of generations, nations, peoples, lands.

God's kingdom is established on justice, but there can be no justice without forgiveness. We think of justice in calculating terms, but to do so is to think too highly of our ability to count. No one knows the heart of a man or the depths of his sin. Sure, we can judge a man by his fruit, and Scripture tells us to do so, but any judgment should be rendered as incomplete and inadequate. We do our best with what we have, and we should abandon any argument that tells us, apart from the Spirit, we can do better than that.

Let's take a quick look at 1 Corinthians 13, the famous love chapter that we so often hear quoted at weddings and read on greeting cards. To describe love, Paul employs some of his most beautiful prose and vivid imagery. But there's a part of chapter 13 that goes largely unquoted. It's the bit about us knowing in part and prophesying in part. We prefer to think of ourselves as people who know and prophesy in full, especially in political and religious matters. But maybe the only way to experience the transcendent beauty of 1 Corinthians 13:1–8 is to believe verse 9. Maybe the humility and grace that come with believing that we know in part open us to the realities of love and unity.

Paul goes on to say that only squabbling children believe that they know in full. But as adults, we must give up childish things, knowing that we see in a mirror dimly. In other words, we don't see ourselves, the situation, or the other person clearly. And that is why we pray, *Dear God, give us eyes to see what's going on here. Spirit of truth, guide us into all Truth, help us rest in the assurance that one day we will know fully as we are fully known. In the meantime, teach us the ways of heaven, that we may be people of faith, hope, and love . . . souls secure in our partial understanding, knowing that we rest in the arms of Truth.*

Not even Jesus would condemn the woman caught in adultery. He told her to step into forgiveness and leave sin behind. We spew meanness, judging and dividing, because we feel judged and fractured. There's a reason why the angels declared peace on earth, goodwill to men. We don't believe that to be true. The Split is too real to us. The curse has done its work. But Jesus sent the Integrator to unify our hearts that we may rise above the hostilities of this age. We pray in the Spirit to know this is true. Prayer connects us with others in ways that don't make sense.

———

My grandfather was a hard man. The sort of person kids shy away from because they always smell like they just took a bath in cigarettes and whiskey. His husky-voiced girlfriend gave me the creeps, but I really liked him and wanted him to like me.

Grandpa Joe was the only person in my family who didn't consider himself a Christ follower. In fact, he was quite vocal about how stupid we all were for believing such nonsense. One time he was in town visiting, and my mom convinced him to go to a service. My mom excitedly told her pastor and specifically asked him to do an altar call so Joe could give his life to Jesus. The pastor obliged and did his best to incite a response from Joe. Well, he got his response. Joe stood up, let out a few cuss words and complaints directed at all the crazy Jesus folk, then stormed out of the church with thousands of people watching him.

That was my grandpa.

Joe was the son of immigrants from Sicily, and his life was a colorful one. He moved out of his parents' home while he was still a boy, lied to join the Navy, and then later played some football in college. There was also a stint with the mob that is still a bit unclear (and we'll keep it that way). He eventually got into building and development and made a small fortune but lost it all in divorces and hard living.

My mom loved him and wanted us to be in his life, so we would drive a couple of hours to visit him for a couple of hours. He always had butterscotch candies in his house, which I loved. My brothers and I would play games on the apartment floor or find a spot to play outside. As I grew a bit older, I noticed that my grandpa never stopped drinking. It also struck me that he was no longer treating my mom in a way that was, well, appropriate for a man to treat any woman, especially his daughter. From that point on, we couldn't visit Grandpa without my dad.

Because my grandpa lived a couple of hours away, we would call him a few days out to make sure our visit worked with his schedule. Following the usual protocol, we planned a visit that worked for Grandpa. But when we arrived that time, there was no greeting, just a note on the door. Apparently, he didn't want to see us and had decided to hit the bottle early at his favorite bar. My mom was livid. It takes a lot of work to go anywhere with a family of six, and we had given up the day just to find some lousy note. She was trying to hold it together, but I could sense her pain. She kept apologizing to the rest of us, as if everything her dad had or hadn't done was somehow her fault. It all just felt wrong and confusing.

My family eventually moved to Colorado, and Grandpa Joe didn't have to worry about us visiting him. In fact, I never saw that apartment again.

More than a decade later, I told my mom that I wanted to visit Joe. I can't really explain why, but I was convinced I could lead him to Jesus. We were flying to Florida for my other grandfather's birthday, so my mom and I, along with my wife and newborn son, made a detour to visit Grandpa Joe, who had been abandoned by his controlling girlfriend and was now living in a center for patients with alcohol-induced dementia.

The last decade had done a lot to my grandpa. He was no longer the strong man that I knew. He had lost his ability to talk, and his eyes would glaze over at times. But during a moment of his lucidity, my mom pulled out pictures from my childhood and pointed to me. He tentatively pointed to me, then the pictures, then back to me, and I smiled and said, "Yes."

In that moment, my mom knew she had his attention. I didn't know it at the time, but she prayed to God and asked for the right words to share with this soul on the threshold of death. Later, she told us the Spirit told her, "Tell him he was a good dad."

That day I watched my mom put her hands around her father and tell him that he was a good dad. I was taken aback by what she said. This was the father who stopped showing her affection when she lost her eye to cancer. This was the father who cheated on her mother and abandoned my mom and her younger brother. As the oldest of my mom's sons, I had seen the most of Joe, I knew the stories, the betrayal and abuse. *Is she really saying what I think she's saying?*

But I denied my need to explain what was happening and let myself enter the moment. Joe began to shake and cry and kiss my mom's hands. The hard man who was forged in a country that didn't want him; whose mother prostituted herself in her own home to support her kids; who saw things in war that he couldn't unsee; who smoked, drank, and womanized from his teenage years traded his pain for a gentleness that I had never seen before.

He then said the only two words we heard from him during that entire visit: "Thank you."

The rock had been crushed.

I knew that was my moment. I walked over and laid my hands on him and prayed the words that he couldn't pray. It was one of the holiest moments of my life. My words were the continuation of Jesus's breath when he breathed the power of forgiveness into his disciples. To this day, I can't hear or share this story without tears running down my cheeks.

My grandpa lived another year and was known as the most pleasant man around. The Spirit had done what only the Spirit can do.

Our Father brought Grandpa Joe home.

To close the chapter, I want to visit a parable that Jesus shared in Matthew 18.

It's a story about two servants and a master. The first servant finds himself hopelessly in debt. To use real numbers, he owes his master roughly 10 billion USD. Yes, your read that right. *Billion* with a *b*.

Having no shot at making good on his debt, the servant begs the master to be patient with him and give him more time to repay the debt. The servant is delusional to think more time is going to make any difference. His chances of sprouting wings and touching the sky are about as good as him paying off the debt. But he begs for time anyway. (In the first century, a man could be imprisoned for such a debt and his family sold into slavery to help offset what he owed.)

What's amazing is the master doesn't give him more time; he knows that his servant can never repay the debt, so he forgives the debt, even though the man didn't request forgiveness. Did you catch that? The man didn't ask for forgiveness. In fact, the man viewed the whole thing as a transaction, which means he left the presence of his master believing that, somehow, he deserved to be forgiven. In some strange way, he calculated that what the master had done was both reasonable and necessary. The debt was an injustice to him, so it was only fitting that he be released of its weight. After all, his master is a rich man and can afford to release him of the debt.

Feeling self-righteous and justified in his freedom, the servant immediately finds a fellow servant who owes him a hundred days' wages and demands that the man pay what he owes. Now, let's be clear—that's no small amount, a third of a year's wages! Imagine if someone owed you a third of your annual salary. In calculable terms, the servant had reason to be upset and pursue recourse. Of course, his fellow servant begs for more time, promising to pay back what he owes, but the unforgiving servant ignores his cries and sentences him to prison until the debt is paid.

When the fellow servants saw what the first servant had done, they reported the details to their master. The master then summoned the unforgiving servant and denounced him as wicked because he refused to forgive his fellow servant. We should note that the master didn't call the servant wicked because he owed a massive debt to him; he called him wicked because he wouldn't participate in mercy and forgiveness. That point is paramount.

The master then delivers the man to torturers, until he should pay off his debt. Most likely, your Bible reads "jailers" instead of "torturers," but "torturers" is the better translation. At that time, the practice of torturing debtors who had been sold into slavery was a way to compel the offender's relatives and friends to purchase their freedom, ending the torture. It was leverage: the offender's friends and family would suffer until the scales were balanced, motivating them to make good on their loved one's debt.

But the problem is, the unforgiving servant's debt is unpayable. Not even the collective efforts of his friends and family will change that—the debt will remain unpayable. This, of course, means that the man's refusal to forgive would cause not only him to suffer but also those closest to him.

Isn't that true of unforgiveness? When we don't forgive, the ones who pay the most are those closest to us. Unforgiveness is a prison, but "to forgive is to set a prisoner free and discover that the prisoner was you."[13]

If we hold on to unforgiveness, we cannot be people of justice, for we will live unaware. When we choose that path, the most merciful thing the Father can do is hand us over to the torturers until our debt is paid. Only in the fire can the unforgiving servant discover that he *cannot* pay his debt. Maybe then he will jettison his "rights" and surrender his broken self to the One who loves him best. Maybe then he will listen to the Voice. As Paul told the Corinthians, "Deliver this man to Satan for the destruction of the flesh, so that his spirit may be saved in the day of the Lord."[14]

> But with you there is forgiveness,
> that you may be feared. (Ps. 130:4)

According to Jesus, forgiveness is a matter of life and death. Being who he was (and is), Jesus knew we'd struggle with the whole forgiveness thing, so he didn't mince words: if we are to hear the Voice, we must receive and extend forgiveness, letting its healing powers refresh our souls, dignify our pain, and direct our words.

13

Trials, Temptations, and Joys

The words of the LORD are pure words,
 like silver refined in a furnace on the ground,
 purified seven times.

Psalm 12:6

A time splashed with interest, wounded with tragedy, crevassed with joy—that's the time that seems long in the memory. Eventlessness has no posts to drape duration on. From nothing to nothing is no time at all.

John Steinbeck, *East of Eden*

friend of mine once told me that she loves the wildernesses of life.
 I told her she was nuts or confused.

"You don't enjoy the wilderness," I replied, "you just like what it does in you."

"No," she responded. "I like the wilderness. That's when I'm most alive, every breath weighed and known; it's when I discover who I am and what I'm capable of. It's where my senses and sense of purpose come alive. It's where faith and hope introduce new facets of God's love."

I wanted to argue with her, but there was something inside me that knew she was right. When most of us look back on our lives, we see that many meaningful and memorable landmarks were forged in pain. We say things like, "I'm thankful for that season now, but I'd never want to live it again." So, we journey ahead, doing our best to make our lives as comfortable, predictable, and safe as possible, unwittingly using our prayers to flatten and dull the landscape of life. We think of praying "Lead us not into temptation, but deliver us from evil" as special language that wards off suffering.

We are, after all, fragile creatures with bodies and minds that are easily broken or bruised. Parachutes and airbags, vaccines and vitamins do their best to preserve and prolong the illusion of immortality. But on most days, something dangerous or disruptive has a way of reminding us that from dust we are and to dust we shall go. As the sage of Ecclesiastes tells us, all our struggle is *hebel,* a vapor subsumed by the winds of existence, lost in the sands of time. Or, as James puts it, "You are a mist that appears for a little time and then vanishes."[1]

All this talk about vapor, dust, and death can depress and repress our spirits, causing us to shrink back and search out the path of least resistance. And when things don't go our way, we're tempted to give ourselves over to fear and rage against God and each other. This fear, which is ultimately the fear of death, is what the writer of Hebrews calls "lifelong slavery."[2] No matter how much we try to escape its grip, this master finds a way to lock us up . . . for good.

But the author of Hebrews also tells us that death and its fear are not ultimate—that Jesus's death destroyed death, delivering us from its fear.[3]

At the Cross, every form of death is swallowed up in Life.

Now we can pray with confidence because the gospel redefines death and life, pain and joy, trial and triumph. What was once our doom (death) has now become our deliverance. For us to know this to be true, though, we must take up our Cross and follow Jesus's downward path, even when it takes us into the fires of suffering. It is only there that we see and know the Consuming Fire, "for everyone," Jesus says, "will be salted with fire."[4] What we don't die to, we'll die from.

> If anyone would come after me, let him deny himself and take up his cross daily and follow me. For whoever would save his life will lose it, but whoever loses his life for my sake will save it. For what does it profit a man if he gains the whole world and loses or forfeits himself? (Luke 9:23–25)

Right now, it's tempting to believe that God at times abandons us to and in our pain.

We've all had those moments—when a loss, or failure, or disappointment, or diagnosis causes our idea of God to break from within. Even Jesus, quoting David, cried out, "Why have you forsaken me?"[5]—making it clear that an intimate part of the human experience is journeying through the sense of abandonment. A truth that marks many of the psalms.

But the story of Scripture also tells us that God is aware of and intimate with our pain, even when we feel the furthest from him. The Father, Son, and Spirit, in their own ways, plumb the depths of human and cosmic suffering. Nothing fractures or breaks without their knowing, and every disorientation of mind, body, and spirit leads to fresh and new orientations: new creations, if you will, that are more permanent and truer than their predecessors.

When Paul writes about the age to come in 1 Corinthians 15, he flatly says that the perishable must put on the imperishable—that God's redemptive process leads us into only more beautiful and authentic realities. In this season, our lives may be sown or spent in weakness, but they will be raised in power. Any conversation about temptations, trials, and joy should keep these promises in mind, for without them, our faith is futile and in vain.

When Jesus teaches us to pray "lead us not into temptation, but deliver us from evil," he is instructing us, through prayer, to contend for and wrestle with different dimensions of pain and deliverance, especially when deliverance feels like a pipe dream considering our present condition or struggle. But for the one who believes and perseveres in prayer, only salvation is final. The day will come when good, in every way, triumphs over evil.

The question is, *How much of that day, and that final reality of blessedness, can and will we participate in here and now?*

The brokenness of our world and the dark powers behind its breaking are at war against the Life and Light of the Saints. That is why we're told to pray for each other in the authority and surety of an everlasting kingdom that is defined by righteousness, peace, and joy. "Deliver us" is a communal request (*us*), a prayer that enjoins us with the struggles and pains of our brothers and sisters, giving us eyes to see and know what we must do on our knees and with our hands. There is an interconnectedness that happens only through prayer, and that is one of the main reasons Scripture urges us to pray for one another.

When we contend for deliverance from evil, we remind ourselves that though we may do battle in evil's domain, we will be delivered from its ultimate destruction and end. That even the enemy's greatest attacks must transform into signposts of God's glory. It is in this struggle against evil, by prayer and action, that we become people of faith, connecting the dots and seeing God's redemptive work around us.

It is "through many tribulations [that] we must enter the kingdom of God."[6]

In Jesus's famous parable of the sower, the same sun that gives life to the seed is also what scorches it. The only difference is the heart in which the seed grows.

Mark's account of this parable makes it clear that the sun is synonymous with the "tribulation or persecution [that] arises on account of the word."[7] In other words, just as the sun rises above a seed, so do tribulation and persecution arise as our hearts glimpse God's kingdom reality. It's worth repeating that the sun nourishes but it also scorches. What gives life also takes it. It is only through prayer that the nuances and subtleties of this truth are grounded in our lives, becoming real to us. When the seed of Truth is rooted in us, the trials that would scorch the seed help it grow and flourish.

The Greek word that is translated "temptation" (*peirasmos*) in The Prayer can also be translated "trial," telling us that trials and temptations, by nature, are inextricably linked. A trial is what happens when our world feels out of joint, becoming an obstacle to our sanity, comfort, security. The temptation that follows is for us to rearrange things to our own design to counteract the trial. We are tempted to use ungodly means to make difficult things right. We feel lonely, so we choose to manipulate and lust. We feel unappreciated, so we give in to pride and self-sufficiency. The trials of life cause us to ask, *Does God really know what he's doing? When it comes to my peace and wellness, maybe I should take matters into my own hands?*

Digging a bit deeper, if we look closely at *peirasmos*, we discover that it's defined as "an attempt to learn the nature or character of something."[8] At first glance, that definition seems strange, but when we think about what trials do in and for us, we realize that they are a place of profound learning and awareness. I once heard suffering defined as what happens when our idea of reality clashes with reality itself. I guess the disorientation is part of the growth.

The question is, What will we do when we're disoriented?

Will we humble ourselves and acknowledge that there's so much about us, God, and this world that needs to be learned and unlearned? Will we allow God to redeem the pain of the trial by allowing it to teach us the true "nature or character of something"? Will we allow prayer to reorient us?

Paul, in one of his letters to the Corinthian church, promises us that

> no temptation has overtaken you that is not common to man. God is faithful, and he will not let you be tempted beyond your ability, but with the temptation he will also provide the way of escape, that you may be able to endure it. (1 Cor. 10:13)

Notice that the escape is not the absence of the temptation but rather our ability to endure or transcend the temptation. In this sense, the temptation (trial) becomes the pathway of godly formation. It is how we grow in character and capacity—all the while knowing that if we face it, we can make it.

When we pray that God would "lead us not into temptation," we are, in a sense, declaring by faith that the temptation or trial is *not the goal or the end*. The Greek word *eis*, translated "into," involves the leading of one to a goal or place, so when we pray lead us *not into*, we are, by faith, acknowledging that the temptation is precisely where we won't be left or left alone. This prayer, and every prayer of its kind, is a reminder to all that there is something beyond and through the temptation. What lies beyond the pain is wholeness, beauty, perfection, promise, intimacy.

If you feel consumed by a temptation or trial, I want to assure you that trial has an end date. The sorrow, pain, disappointment, and hopelessness that feel all-consuming and never-ending must bow a knee to God's eternal and perfecting Love, a love that becomes real to us through the power of faith and hope. That is why James could write, "Count it all joy, my brothers and sisters, when you meet trials of various kinds, for you know that the testing of your faith produces steadfastness. And let steadfastness have its full effect, that you may be perfect and complete, lacking in nothing."[9]

Though sorrow may claim the night, joy will come with the dawn.

Before we go any further, it's important to make it clear that we don't need to seek out trials and testing. They have a way of finding us and delivering us from our doubts, fears, insecurities, and pride. Referring back to the parable of the sower, it is not our responsibility nor are we capable of making the sun rise for the sake of our souls.

Only a religious spirit seeks and creates its own affliction. By doing so, it puts us in charge of our process. God doesn't need you to make it hard on yourself. The frailty and brokenness of this age will provide struggle enough, a struggle that is no match for the Spirit of grace, the One who powers us through every trial.

Peter, a man who knew great suffering, wrote that "after you have suffered a little while, the *God of all grace*, who has called you to his eternal glory in Christ, will himself restore, confirm, strengthen, and establish you."[10] Notice that Peter describes the suffering as "a little while." In the perspective of eternity, the suffering is a vapor, but God has an eternal glory that he *himself* will give to us. What a promise!

When we pray in and through promises like that one, we are filled with faith and find the courage and ability to see things as they truly are, "for faith is not a leap out of the everyday but a plunge into its depth."[11] A plunge into what's most real about our past, present, and future.

None of this is easy, but what is easy is rarely what is best or meaningful. Even Jesus sweat blood as he had words with the Father and stared down the suffering to come. In the garden of rebirth, the Son asked if there was another way, while submitting to the brokenly human (but redemptively divine) process of becoming what we already are through pain and suffering, making it clear that prayer is not a mechanism to escape the moment; it is the pathway into and through the moment.

The Father is near the brokenhearted. The pain cannot silence the Voice.

When Scripture mentions pain and sorrow, it has a curious way of also lifting our eyes to the promise of joy, even going so far as to say that the joy of the Lord is our strength in the trial.[12]

Joy is one of those heavenly qualities, the kind that doesn't make much sense unless you're in on the great secret. It's not the same as happiness, which is pretty easy to understand. Good things happen, we're happy. Circumstances are favorable, we're happy. But I think of joy as defiant, as the most reasonable unreasonableness. I guess I'm borrowing that language from Paul:

> Rejoice in the Lord always; again I will say, rejoice. Let your *reasonableness* be known to everyone. The Lord is at hand. (Phil. 4:4–5, emphasis mine)

This is one of those moments in Scripture where we must ask ourselves if Paul's lost it. The man is, after all, in a prison, writing on joy. The irony. Maybe he's been beaten with rods one too many times. Or could he be writing this with clenched teeth and a bit of a bite on his tongue?

As we take a closer look at these verses, though, we see that this isn't a forced sentiment; these verses, and the extended thought that they're a part of, have beautiful and authentic symmetry.

First, we're told to rejoice always, not saving our joy for when things are good or when things work out how we want. And just in case we thought it was a slip of the pen, he repeats the instruction: "Again I will say, rejoice."

Okay, Paul, we're listening.

What comes next is almost as baffling: "Let your reasonableness be known to everyone." In other words, Paul is saying it is unreasonable not to participate in joy. Or to put it differently, anything that is not energized by joy is unreasonable.

If you're anything like me, you're probably thinking, *Surely, there must be exceptions*, but "always" leaves no room for caveats. The most reasonable thing we can do, always, is to be people of joy.

So how does that work? How can we be full of joy always?

Well, Paul doesn't intend to leave us in the dark. He goes on to write, "The Lord is at hand." For him, the promise of God's nearness brings joy. A promise that, in some ways, seems too simple to be of any help. But the simple sort are usually the best, and, for Paul, we can live in constant joy simply because the King and the kingdom are always at hand. This joy is not confined to the transience of the everyday; it is rooted in the eternal Truth that what is temporal and terrifying will eventually yield to the peace and purpose of God's everlasting kingdom.

We, by the power of God's Spirit, the One who transcends time, can find the joy of the kingdom even within today's pain. We can let our sorrow be swallowed by the joy to come, without denying the pain of the moment. The most mature emotions are, actually, what emerge from two truths that are held in tension. We rejoice because God's "new world is to be born through our present pain and travail."[13] The pain is part of the birth, an indicator that new life is indeed about to break forth.

Somehow joy is what carries us from now to then, from the pain into the promise. Joy has a way of opening our eyes and ears to what is ultimately true. It was joy, after all, that energized Jesus's journey to the Cross. It's the only reasonable response if we believe what Jesus and Paul say.

But where do we find the strength to believe such joy is possible? How do we cultivate a faith in the unseen that is more real than the prison of pain before our eyes? How can we hear the Voice among our cries of desperation? How do we know that the Lord is indeed "at hand"?

Paul gives us the answer. In fact, he gives it to us multiple times, in different letters. Let's look at three accounts here. Notice that in each of these letters, the path of joy comes with prayer.

> Rejoice in the Lord always; again I will say, rejoice. . . . Do not be anxious about anything, but in everything *by prayer* and supplication with thanksgiving let your requests be made known to God. (Phil. 4:4, 6, emphasis mine)

> Rejoice in hope, be patient in tribulation, be *constant in prayer.* (Rom. 12:12, emphasis mine)

> Rejoice always, *pray without ceasing,* give thanks in all circumstances. (1 Thess. 5:16–18, emphasis mine)

Prayer is what connects us to what's really happening. Those who are constant in prayer just see things differently and can't help but live with a bit of a twinkle in their eye and gratitude in their hearts, no matter what life throws their way. This way of living is not built on delusion, denial, or ignorance. Connected with the heart of the world, they can't help but feel loss and pain deeper than anyone else, and that's why they are the best at traveling with others into and through affliction.[14]

We can and should mourn death and loss, but that doesn't mean we have to hold on to them (or be held by them) with an iron grip. For now, joy and mourning must go together because joy knows that death must come and go first. That in our present pain and trial, we are being reborn—for the age to come, yes, but also for the present moment. Not even the sting of death can steal our joy, for while joy is eternal, death folds in on itself, losing its power.

Therefore, we can give thanks in all circumstances. Notice, though, that Paul doesn't say that we give thanks *for* all circumstances. We're not grateful for the pain itself, but we know it too will be redeemed, and for that we are thankful. Our gratitude is based on God's faithfulness and character, not our moment of trial or temptation. We have assurance that God himself will deliver us from every trial, and that's reason enough for joy.

Much of what I've written may seem absurd or foreign to you, and that's because we've largely understated the importance and centrality of joy in the life of the Christ follower. Joy is often seen as juvenile or unbecoming of those who take life and work seriously. But right in the middle of navigating a serious argument about matters of eating and drinking, points of contention that people have lost relationships to, Paul reminds us that the kingdom of God isn't about that stuff, but rather about righteousness, peace, and joy in the Holy Spirit.[15]

The way Paul uses *righteousness* in his letter to the Romans conveys the idea of familial belonging or togetherness. And because we belong together—because God has made us for himself and each other, creating us differently to make us complementary—we can be at peace with God and man. We don't have to get bent out of shape trying to prove what we already are or disprove what the other isn't. And because we live a life of righteousness and peace, the only reasonable thing for us to do is be people of joy, which unites our hearts and connects our lives.

Let's not forget that Jesus told us to abide or dwell in the reality of his love, the love that he shares with the Father, that his joy may be in us and that our joy may be full.[16] The life of the kingdom is a life of joy. A return to Eden, which literally means en*joy*ment or delight, is the way of the kingdom. Do you think it's any accident that God uses celebratory and feasting (joy) language to describe the kingdom?

We may receive the word—the seed—in much affliction, but we can and must do so with the joy of the Spirit.[17] There's a reason why the fruit of the Spirit is love working itself out in joy, among other attributes. I do love that the first and last expression of the fruit of the Spirit (summed up in love) are joy and self-control. Don't tell me that God doesn't have a sense of humor. The joyful can have self-control and the self-controlled must have joy. Otherwise, we get all this wrong. Just think of the number of people who've denied the reality of our faith because of the absence of our joy.

In his book *He That Is Spiritual*, Lewis Sperry Chafer took a swing at the anti-joy sentiment commonly held among the spiritually elite. "Spirituality is not a pious pose. It is not a 'Thou Shalt not'; it is 'Thou shalt.' It flings open the doors into the eternal blessedness, energies, and resources of God. It is a serious thing to remove the element of relaxation and play from any life. We cannot be normal physically, mentally, or spiritually if we neglect this vital factor in human life. God has provided that our joy shall be full."[18]

When the fires of life rage, whether they be internal or external, it's easy to believe that we've done this to ourselves. We forgot to turn the stove off, so of course the house burned to the ground. The sirens scream, everything's lost, and it's all our fault. Or maybe we're one of those who vehemently deny complicity, even as we stand there with matches or smoking gun in hand. There's always someone else to blame for the mess; we're just victims of the madness.

The truth is we are both villain and victim. We are born into a broken world, but we also do our own share of breaking. And deep down, we know this to be true.

Maybe you're someone who believes you are beyond hope—that the trials, testing, and tribulation of life are poetic justice. They belong to you, and you to them, so why should you pray for deliverance when the evil is of your own making? You won't have words with God because you don't think he should stoop into your mess.

But the truth is, God reunites you to himself, even when it seems like life is destroying you.

The question is, Will we let go of everything that is anti-life and, therefore, anti-God? The Father, in his mercy, tries our hearts and leads us into the dark night of the soul. In this place of surrender, the pain of our brokenness helps deliver us from self-righteousness and self-sufficiency, and we are compelled to behold—and be held by—the Father again, seeing the righteous face of God, and hearing the Voice in fresh ways.

Throughout Scripture we see what Eugene Peterson calls the great paradox of God's judgment, that evil becomes fuel in the furnace of salvation.[19] It's tempting to believe that any evil dwells beyond the reach of God's sovereignty. But God is the Lord over evil, and we are promised deliverance from its grip, whatever form evil may take.

We participated in the corruption of this world, and God has invited us to join in its salvation. To storm the gates of hell, as Jesus put it.[20] Our mission is not possible, however, if we cower to or deny evil. When it's all said and done, in Christ, we triumph over death and Hades. So we mustn't shrink back in our prayers. The Father will deliver us from evil. That is the vision of godly hope, the power of faith, and the surety of Love.

There's a moment in the small book of Joel when the day of judgment was on the people. Judgment came in the form of an army, one that Scripture describes as being of incalculable darkness and despair.[21] This army is an agent of God's judgment.

As the book unfolds, it seems like there is no hope in sight. The people have sinned, and they must face the evil spawn of their sins. But in the twelfth verse of the second chapter, the narrative takes a hard turn. With three words, God changes everything. Yet. Even. Now.

The people are told that if they repent, turn from their ways, and cry out to God, "yet even now" he will transform the disaster and deliver them from themselves. To quote the prophet, "Who knows whether he will not turn . . . and leave a blessing behind him?"[22] A blessing in the wake of judgment. Triumph on the heels of temptation.

This is our God. There is none like him. When trials weigh you down and evil surrounds you, he wants you to have words with him. For yet even now, he has words of life for you.

Lead us not into temptation . . . deliver us from evil.

14

In the Name

Who has ascended to heaven and come down?
Who has gathered the wind in his fists?
Who has wrapped up the waters in a garment?
Who has established all the ends of the earth?
What is his name, and what is his son's name?
Surely you know!

Proverbs 30:4

Hallowed be your name.

Luke 11:2

When we talk with others, we like to know their names. There's just something about names that makes people real. Conversations tend to get awkward when names aren't exchanged or are forgotten, not to mention it's considered rude not to care enough to know or remember a name. Pronouns and impersonal identifiers can take us only so far. If a connection is to be made, names must be exchanged.

So what does any of this have to do with prayer? Apparently, everything. Jesus told us to pray *in his name*; I guess that's the reason so many prayers end with "in Jesus's name." But beyond being a nice way to close a prayer and transition to whatever's next, we should ask ourselves, *What does it mean to pray in Jesus's name?*

There's a famous account in Scripture that involves a man, a bush, and a name. Moses was just doing what he did every day, herding sheep and such, when suddenly he saw a burning bush that wasn't consumed. Bushes are supposed to burn, so Moses rejected his normal routine to see this great sight. There's a good chance you know the story, so I won't share all the details, but there's a moment in the story that's crucial to our understanding of God's name and what it means to pray in the Name.

Speaking out of the bush, the Voice introduces himself and tells Moses,

I am the God [Elohim] of your father. (Exod. 3:6)

The thing is, though, "Elohim" was a bit generic, used similarly to how we use the term *god* or *gods* today. As excited as Moses was that God was speaking to him, he wanted to know more about the One behind the Voice, especially since he, a criminal and outcast who struggled to speak, was being asked to reintroduce a nation to the God who had abandoned them to slavery for hundreds of years. For Moses, "Elohim" wasn't going to cut it: he wanted more.

If . . . the people of Israel . . . ask me, "What is his name?" what shall I say to them? (Exod. 3:13)

There's a subtlety in the text here that isn't captured by the English translation. When Moses asks, "What (*mah*) is his name?" the word translated "what" is different from the Hebrew pronoun (*mi*) that would typically be used when asking for a name. To use *mah* is to travel beyond mere sounds and inquire into the nature or meaning or substance of a name. It is to seek out what defines a person. It's as if Moses asked God, "Who and what are you, really?"

The Voice famously responds, "I will be as I will be," or, "I AM WHO I AM."[1]

In other words, God promises that his name is an unfolding certainty, sufficient for every moment or situation, and, yes, that includes the deliverance and salvation of nations. For Moses, on that day, the Name held the promise that God's power and presence permeated every place, even Egypt. A fact that would soon be evident through many signs and wonders, triumphs and trials. According to God, this name would "be remembered throughout all generations,"[2] for in it all things live and move and have their being.

For much of this book, when we've looked at how Jesus taught us to pray, we've visited Matthew's Gospel and its version of the Lord's Prayer. Matthew's version is the one we liturgize and pray, but there's a nuance in Luke's Gospel that helps us yield our prayers to the Name behind the Voice.

In both Matthew's and Luke's Gospels, the center and strength of The Prayer lies in the character or nature of God. He is Father and the Holy One—hallowed be *your name*—and any prayer must be built on this eternal foundation. The two accounts may differ in style, but they both agree that God's name is the substance of prayer. Luke, however, takes this revelation a step further by following The Prayer with a story, challenging us to take a fresh look at the Name.

We're going to geek in Greek for a moment. I promise it'll be worth it.

This story (it's actually a parable) has two main characters: a sleeping father and a friend in need. In Greek, this parable is built as two inverted stanzas with six units each, and the symmetry is both beautiful and intentional. The first stanza (Luke 11:5–9) sets up a hypothetical situation. Paraphrased, it could read something like this,

> Can any one of you imagine having a friend and going to him at midnight with a sacred request for a guest, and that friend then offers silly excuses and tells you that he can't get up and give you anything?

Luke would expect the reader to respond, "Of course not. That would be all wrong." We should remember that to deny such a request in Luke's world would dishonor everyone involved. The guest was the responsibility of the community; both the sleeper and the requester were expected to respond as they could. The community's honor—their name—would be at stake. If they failed to be hospitable, they would all be objects of shame.

After laying out this absurd scenario, Luke moves into the second stanza, setting the stage for his crucial point. Here's a breakdown of the stanza, with each of the six units placed on its own line. For clarity's sake, I've included the subject of each unit in parentheses as well, the subject being the one who the unit is ultimately about:

If he will not give to him (the sleeper)
    Having arisen (the sleeper)
        Because of being a friend of his (the sleeper)
        But because of his *anaideia* (the sleeper)
    He will arise (the sleeper)
    And will give him whatever he needs. (the sleeper)

Notice the linguistic and stylistic pattern. Each of these units should place the action on the sleeper, the one who, in this parable, represents God and how he responds to our prayers. The challenge is most translations make a mess of this passage because they don't know what to do with *anaideia*, a Greek word found in the fourth unit.[3] This word is often mistranslated as persistence or shamelessness, so it's applied to the requester (us) because it would be strange, in this context, for God (the sleeper) to be the persistent one.

Recent scholarship has revealed, however, that *anaideia* has nothing to do with the positive or negative qualities of persistence.[4] Now, is it good to be persistent in prayer? Absolutely. Persistence prepares us for the petition. But that's not the point of this parable, nor of the greater thought surrounding it. The word *anaideia* actually conveys the avoidance of shame, making it equivalent with the matter of honor, which just so happens to be the thematic climax of both stanzas. Luke, in both stanzas, is setting up a scenario that if mishandled will bring dishonor and shame to all the parable's characters.

With that in mind, let's turn to the mistake of making the requester (us) the subject of the fourth unit. When it comes to prayer, we tend to make ourselves the hero (or villain) of the story. *If only I would've prayed more or harder or differently.* But this parable, again, isn't ultimately about us. Yes, we must ask, seek, and contend for the sake of his name, but Jesus is using this parable to give us insight into the hallowed nature of God, a God who himself promises to give us not just what we ask for but everything that we need. The symmetry of the other five units makes it clear that when it comes to prayer, the question of honor lies with God. It's his name that is on the line. For Luke, the word *anaideia* tells the story of God's honor, his word. Not ours.[5]

Jesus's big point here culminates in the promise that if evil neighbors will lose some sleep to avoid shame, how much more will the heavenly Father give the Holy Spirit to those who ask him (v. 13)! In other words, God's Spirit, his very life, if you will, is promised to those who dare to know, seek, understand, ask. To those who call on his name.

When we pray "in Jesus's name" we are not using magical language that somehow ensures that our prayers are answered. Rather, when we pray in his name, we are confronting the dangerous yet comforting certainty that "he is who he is," and that his every response, whatever form the response may take, is for the sake or honor of his name.

Much has been believed about God, his nature, and his name, but Jesus tells us that the Father is seen through him. Jesus is perfectly intimate with the Name, for the Name is his own: "I and the Father are one."[6] And he tells us that by praying in the Name we venture into the reality, authority, and surety of the One who "upholds the universe by the word of his power."[7]

When we pray, "Hallowed be your name," we remind ourselves that God is both immanent and transcendent. Now and then. Here and there. The Triune God is of one essence or one name, while operating as distinct persons. The three persons of God are the heart of the Divine Dance, their movements giving life to all who are grasped by their name. We are to be one with the Father, as the Son and Spirit are one with him. That was the Son's prayer, remember?

> Holy Father, keep them in *your name*, which you have given me, that they may be one, even as we are one. (John 17:11, emphasis mine)

We participate in this union through prayer, which awakens us to how God's eternal love unfolds in our everyday life. Even the original meaning of the word *theology* conveyed a union with God through prayer. Praying in Jesus's name places the Mystery of "I will be who I will be" before our eyes, so we can learn to see the One who never ceases to work on our behalf and hear the Voice that never stops calling. Jesus said that the Holy Spirit would be sent in both his and the Father's name, that the Spirit of truth would ground us in the Truth, helping us understand that which is beyond us, giving us courage to take a step of faith and join the Dance. To open the conversation so we can hear the words we most long to hear.

The Spirit by whom we pray is Lord of the Canyon.

The Son in whom we pray is Lord of the Temple.

The Father to whom we pray is Lord of the Dance.

It is a prayer of faith, faith in the triune nature of God, revealed in the Son and sustained by the Spirit, that leads us to what is ultimately true about the Father. "It is through the Spirit," wrote Andrew Murray, "that the Name, which is above every name in heaven, will take the place of supremacy in our hearts and life too."[8]

Jesus is God's Word. The One in whom every true word finds a home. We have life in his name because his name has become our own: He is the Holy One, and we are holy ones. He is the Beloved Son, and we are his brothers and sisters, beloved by the Father. To the degree that we understand this to be true, we can pray in the authority and authenticity and permanency of his name.

Jesus's name, the Name that is above every other name, has the final say on matters of life and death, us and them, mercy and judgment, grace and truth. His name is what has always been true about God: Father, Son, and Spirit. The Name of God unfolds in the biblical narrative, taking on perfect form and flesh in Jesus of Nazareth—the One in whom we pray is the intersection of what is ultimately true about God and us. To pray in the Name is to confront any lie in any place that would try to tell us otherwise, for all deception is and will be undone by his name.

The world started with the Word, the *logos* or Truth of all things. Then Truth tabernacled or dwelt with us, merging time and space, immanence and transcendence, God and man. As we pray in the Name, God's kingdom becomes clearer to us. We see its evidence even in the darkness of the canyon. Even in pain, it's through praying in the Name that we learn what is ultimately true about God, ourselves, and others. That is why life is in the Name.

———

The One who is Life asked his followers, "Who do you say that I am?"[9]

There were many opinions on what Jesus should be called: heretic, teacher, charlatan, and prophet, to name a few. But Jesus looked to those closest to him, asking them what name they would assign to the miracle-working craftsman from Nazareth.

That's when Simon famously blurted out, "You are the Christ, the Son of the living God."[10] Or the son of I AM (the Name). Jesus goes on to tell Simon that such revelation was beyond man and could come only from the Father in heaven. He also gives Simon the name Peter, declaring that the *ekklesia* ("church") would be built on both him and this revelation. That the *ekklesia* would be those who are called by the Name. The word *ekklesia* comes from the Greek *ek* ("origin") and *kaleo* ("to name or call"); literally, it conveys the idea of us being called out and renamed according to origin, called back to the family of God.

Jesus then declares that the gates of hell—embodying the blindness of idolatry, sin, accusation—shall not prevail against this revelation. We are to storm the darkness because we are children of the Light. Our confidence is in the banner of his name, the Name that has become our own, for we too are reborn from above. We have the keys to the kingdom. No gate can remain shut to us when we live and pray in the power of his name.

In the Name there is

Life (John 20:31)
Forgiveness (Acts 2:38)
Restoration (Ps. 23:3)
Healing (Acts 3:6)
Strength (Mark 9:39)
Authority (Phil. 2:10)
Power (Ps. 106:8)
Love (1 John 3:23)

Boldness (Acts 9:27)

Salvation (1 Cor. 1:2)

Deliverance (Acts 16:18)

Confidence (Acts 21:13)

Unity (1 Cor. 1:10)

Justification (1 Cor. 6:11)

Gratitude (Col. 3:17)

Glory (2 Thess. 1:12) . . . the Name is everything we need.

This revelation, growing in his heart, would lead Peter to write that we are now partakers of the divine nature.[11] This blessed certainty would cause John to pen that God's *sperma* (seed) abides in us, redeeming and restoring us as sons and daughters.[12] I guess they finally got it when Jesus told them that he must ascend to "my father and your father."[13] Because we belong to the Name and the Name to us, we carry it through the darkness, where every shadow must transform into signposts of glory. We belong to the Name because we are temple people, caught up in the Dance that knows no bounds. For,

> All the ends of the earth shall remember
> and turn to the LORD,
> and all the families of the nations
> shall worship before you. (Ps. 22:27)

Every time we pray in the Name, we claim our inheritance as sons and daughters, the Saints who are stewards of God's good creation. Creation is waiting on tiptoe for us to know this is true. Even now, it lends its voice to the song and moves toward the Dance.

The heavens declare the glory of God. . . .
Their voice goes out through all the earth,
  and their words to the end of the world. (Ps. 19:1, 4)

With confidence, we can open the conversation, taking courage to see every moment as holy.

I love what Jesus says about what happens when we gather in his name: "where two or three are gathered in my name, there am I among them."[14] There's cosmic resonance when we gather in his name, for the communion of the Spirit is with us always. God's Voice is never silent. It speaks through persons and places, in silence and sound. It speaks in mystery and clarity, for both are necessary now. God doesn't just hear our words. He's in them: teaching us how to articulate what is most true about us, our hope, our pain, our longings, our lack. We can, by the Spirit's integrating power, be those who join the Dance, even in the canyon.

If the essence of prayer is the act of God working in us and raising our whole being to himself, which it is, then by praying in the Name, we yield to the immensity of that "impossible" act, the miracle of God recreating us in the power of I AM.

The Voice has the final say over our lives, and he calls us his own. His name is above every other name—sin and shame, disease and disaster, the secular and the sacred. The Word breathes life into our words, revealing what they mean in the light of eternity. As C. S. Lewis writes, "I know now, Lord, why you utter no answer. You are yourself the answer. Before your face questions die away. What other answer would suffice? Only words, words; to be led out to battle against other words."[15]

To know the Name is to participate in the power and permanence of God.

The God who is everywhere.
The God who sees.
The God who provides.
The God who heals.
The God who forgives.
The God who fights for us.
The God who speaks.

To pray in the Name is to give the Voice, who has a name, the final Word.

Author's Note

I have spent years working on this book, yet I have the sense that my work has just begun. My heart and hands are energized by a desire to know in greater measure the integrated life of intimacy with God, the promise of shalom, the way of the Dance, and to help others do the same.

For that reason, I'd like to open the conversation with you, dear reader, and invite you to reach out to me with any thoughts, stories, and ideas for serving and supporting others in their pursuit of connecting with God. I'd also love to hear how and why this book spoke to you. I am a bit reclusive and don't spend much time on social platforms, but here is my personal email address. I welcome your words.

Sincerely,
Addison D. Bevere
addison@wordswithgod.org

Acknowledgments

To the love of my life and keeper of most of my words, this book wouldn't have happened without you, Juli. (That Mother's Day at Dollywood was everything to me.) It's the joy of my life to call myself yours and travel this road with you. "Thank you" is inadequate.

To my children, Asher, Sophia, Elizabeth, and Augustus, thank you for your patience, support, and willingness to answer my questions and share your stories. You have no idea how much your nightly prayers and encouraging words mean to me. I love being your father.

To Andrea, your positivity and steadfastness throughout this project astounded me. "Trust the process." And your idea to separate the manuscript into three parts broke the dam, releasing the final chapters. It's an honor to count myself as one of your authors.

To my parents, John and Lisa, you modeled prayer and prayerfulness in beautifully different ways. Thank you for pioneering and forging new pathways for those who come behind you. Your faithfulness to God and each other is inspiring.

To my brothers, Austin, J. Alexander, and Arden, thank you for being the best brothers anyone could ask for. Much of who I am today has been shaped by and in your presence.

To Chris, Scott, Heather, and my comrades at Messenger International, working and praying with you has enlarged my world. Thank you for all the support, feedback, and creativity that you invested in this project. It wouldn't have happened without you.

To Jen, Mark, Brianna, Laura, Eileen, Sadina, Julie, and the team at Baker, your excitement about and commitment to this book made all the difference. I loved our collaboration and am so grateful for the way you guided this work into its finished form.

To Esther and the team at the FEDD Agency, this book has life because of your faith, support, and advocacy. Thank you for making the impossible, possible. All your trips, calls, emails, and texts paved the road here. We did it!

To my endorsers, thank you for your kind, personal, and generous words. Each of you has a lot of demands placed on your time, so your investment of words speaks volumes to me.

To my dear friends, family, and mentors not mentioned above, the need for brevity isn't my friend here, so I must refrain from listing names. (Not to mention I'm terrified by the idea of missing someone who should be mentioned.) But you know who you are, and I am profoundly grateful that God has intertwined our lives. Thank you for being my people.

Notes

Chapter 1 The Voice

1. Karl Barth, *Watch for the Light* (Walden, NY: Plough Publishing, 2014), 137.
2. Paraphrase of John 12:28–30.
3. See Gen. 3 and Rom. 8.
4. Gary V. Smith, *The New American Commentary: Isaiah 1–39, Volume 15A (New American Commentary) (Volume 15)* (Nashville: Holman Reference, 2007), 191.
5. Rom. 8:26–27, 34.
6. See 1 Cor. 2:16.

Chapter 2 Into Silence

1. See Matt. 11:28–30.
2. My paraphrase of Judg. 6:11–13.
3. Rom. 4:13–25.
4. Phil. 2:12–13.
5. Rom. 8:26.
6. See Eccles. 3:11.
7. See examples in Heb. 11.

Chapter 3 The Prayer

1. Yonat Shimron, "Most Americans Believe in a Higher Power, but Not Always in the God of the Bible," *Washington Post*, April 25, 2018, https://www

.washingtonpost.com/news/acts-of-faith/wp/2018/04/25/most-americans
-believe-in-a-higher-power-but-not-always-in-the-god-of-the-bible/.

2. Eugene Peterson, *As Kingfishers Catch Fire: A Conversation on the
Ways of God Formed by the Words of God* (Colorado Springs: Waterbrook,
2017), 285.

3. Elizabeth Barrett Browning, *Aurora Leigh*, book 7 (1856).

4. See Exod. 19.

5. Exod. 20:21.

6. See Rom. 8:1–4; 2 Cor. 3:4–6.

7. See Exod. 19:6.

8. Also see Pss. 40:6–8; 50:16–17; Isa. 1; Hosea 6; Amos 5; and Jesus's
comment about how he desires mercy instead of sacrifice in Matt. 9:13; 12:7.

9. See Matt. 23:4; Prov. 29:18.

10. Tertullian, Cyprian, and Origen, *On the Lord's Prayer: St. Vladimir's
Seminary Press Popular Patristics Series*, trans. Alistair Stewart-Sykes (Yonkers, NY: St. Vladimir's Seminary Press, 2004), 42.

11. Paul Tillich, *The New Being* (Lincoln: Bison Books, 2005), 148.

Chapter 4 What We Call God

1. N. T. Wright, *The Lord and His Prayer* (Grand Rapids: Eerdmans,
2014), 10.

2. Matt. 7:11.

3. Bauer, W., F. W. Danker, W. F. Arndt, and F. W. Gingrich, *Greek-
English Lexicon of the New Testament and Other Early Christian Literature*,
3rd ed. (Chicago: University of Chicago Press, 2000), s.v. *ponēros*.

4. See Luke 20:18.

5. See Acts 14:22.

6. See John 16:33.

7. Matt. 23:9.

8. Heb. 4:12.

9. See Heb. 2:11; 4:14–16.

10. Matt. 5:4.

11. John 14:9; Col. 1:19.

12. Matt. 4:3, 6.

13. John 17:23, 26.

14. John 3:16.

15. John 13:35.

16. See John 5:19.

17. John 1:12, emphasis mine.

Chapter 5 Seeing the Kingdom

1. N. T. Wright, *Galatians: Commentaries for Christian Formation* (Grand Rapids: Eerdmans, 2021), 12.

2. See John 1:29–34, 35–52; 2:1–12, 13–22.

3. John 3:2.

4. Mark 11:17.

5. See 1 Cor. 4.

6. Matt. 23:13.

7. Paraphrase of Matt. 23:15.

8. John 12:31–33.

9. Tillich, *The New Being*, 177.

10. John 2:19.

11. See 1 Cor. 3:16–17.

12. Luke 17:21 NKJV.

13. Gal. 3:27–29.

14. Dallas Willard, *The Spirit of the Disciplines: Understanding How God Changes Lives* (New York: HarperCollins, 1988), 214.

15. See Matt. 23:8–12.

16. See 2 Cor. 5:17–20.

17. John 3:17.

18. Mark 8:18.

19. See Matt. 6:22–23.

20. John 1:4.

21. See vv. 18, 22, and 27.

Chapter 6 Opening the Conversation

1. See Ps. 37:23 NLT.

2. See 1 Cor. 10:31.

3. See Ps. 139:18.

4. See John 5:19.

5. Willard, *The Spirit of the Disciplines*, 31.

6. See 1 Cor. 6:15–20.

7. 1 Tim. 4:7–8.

8. Acts 24:16.

9. This is the translation used in Acts 24:16 KJV.

10. Phil. 2:12.

11. 2 Cor. 7:1.

12. Matt. 26:41.

13. 1 John 2:29; 3:7; 3:10.

14. Dallas Willard, *The Great Omission: Reclaiming Jesus's Essential Teachings on Discipleship* (New York: HarperCollins, 2006), 61.

15. See James 1:21.

16. John 1:1, 14.

17. Willard, *The Spirit of the Disciplines*, 138.

18. Rev. 12:11.

19. See Ps. 116:17.

20. Prov. 4:26.

21. James Allen, *As A Man Thinketh* (Longmeadow Press, 1993), 30.

22. See Rom. 12:2.

23. See 2 Cor. 10:5.

Chapter 7 The Integrator

1. Carl R. Trueman, *The Rise and Triumph of the Modern Self: Cultural Amnesia, Expressive Individualism, and the Road to Sexual Revolution* (Wheaton: Crossway, 2020), 141.

2. Ps. 19:1–2.

3. See 2 Cor. 3:17–18.

4. See Gal. 5:22–23.

5. Rudolf Otto, *The Idea of the Holy* (Oxford University Press, 1958), ch. 4.

6. Isa. 6:3.

7. C. S. Lewis, *Mere Christianity* from *The Complete C. S. Lewis Signature Classics Collection* (New York: HarperOne, 2002), 143.

8. Acts 17:28.

9. J. B. Phillips, *New Testament Christianity* (New York: Macmillan, third printing, 1964), 19.

10. John 17:21.

11. See 2 Cor. 3:7.

12. John 13:35 NIV.

13. John 20:22.

14. See 1 John 3:24; 4:13.

15. Rom. 5:5.

Chapter 8 I Am Here

1. Heb. 2:14–15.

2. See Luke 9; 1 Corinthians 15.

3. Steve Bradt, "Wandering mind not a happy mind," *The Harvard Gazette*, November 11, 2010, https://news.harvard.edu/gazette/story/2010/11/wandering-mind-not-a-happy-mind/.

4. V. 2.

5. Thomas M. Sterner, *Fully Engaged: Using the Practicing Mind in Daily Life* (Novato, CA: New World Library, 2016), 72.

6. Phil. 4:5–6.

7. Paraphrased from Augustine, *Confessions*.

Chapter 9 How Should We Ask?

1. See Matt. 6:7–8.

2. See v. 8.

3. See 1 Tim. 4:16.

4. See Matt. 13:12.

5. Tertullian, Cyprian, and Origen, *On the Lord's Prayer*, 42.

6. See John 15:1–11.

7. See Matt. 7:7–11; Luke 11:10–13.

8. Rabbi Jonathan Sacks, *Morality: Restoring the Common Good in Divided Times* (New York: Basic Books, 2020), 63.

9. N. T. Wright, *The Lord and His Prayer*, 23.

10. See Ps. 37:25.

Chapter 10 Confession, Sin, and Conscience

1. Lisa Bevere, *Fiercely Loved: God's Wild Thoughts About You* (Grand Rapids: Revell, 2022).

2. See Heb. 4:16.

3. See James 5:16.

4. 1 Cor. 9:21; James 1:25.

5. Vv. 1–2.

6. Matt. 23:23.

7. See Luke 12:12.

8. Lewis, *Mere Christianity*. Lewis unpacks this idea in book 1, chapter 1.

9. Vv. 4, 7.

Chapter 11 Me to We

1. Paraphrased from Koyama Kosuke, *Three Mile an Hour God* (Norwich, UK: SCM Press, 2021), 23.

2. Thomas Merton, *No Man Is an Island* (New York: HarperOne, 2002), 64.

3. Matt. 12:39.

4. Jon. 1:9.

5. See Jon. 3:1.

6. Jon. 3:3.

7. Jon. 4:1.

8. Jon. 4:2 (emphasis mine).

9. 2 Kings 14:25.

10. Jon. 4:9.

11. John 10:16.

12. Eph. 4:3.

13. See Eph. 2:14–16.

14. See Col. 1:26.

15. Eph. 4:4–6.

16. Eph. 3:14–15.

17. See 2 Cor. 5:19.

18. See Acts 1:1–11.

19. Acts 1:6.

20. Acts 1:8.

21. See Exod. 34:22.

22. 2 Cor. 3:3.

23. See Matt. 5:44.

24. Eph. 6:12.

25. Eph. 6:18.

26. Mother Teresa, "Acceptance Speech," The Nobel Peace Prize 1979, The Nobel Prize, December 10, 1979, https://www.nobelprize.org/prizes/peace/1979/teresa/acceptance-speech/.

27. Howard Thurman, *The Inward Journey* (Richmond, IN: Friends United Press, 2007), 105.

28. Adapted from Howard Thurman, *Jesus and the Disinherited* (Boston: Beacon Press, 1976), 85.

Chapter 12 Forgiveness

1. The first martyr mentioned after Jesus's ascension.

2. Acts 7:55.

3. Acts 6:10.

4. Tom Wright, *Mark for Everyone* (London: Society for Promoting Christian Knowledge , 2004), 16–17. Wright once said,

> Most people don't realize that this was probably Jesus' own house. He had moved to Capernaum from Nazareth; the point of the first two verses is that when Jesus returned from his short preaching trip around the neighbouring villages, he found crowds pressing around the door as though he were a movie star or well-known footballer. Jesus himself was the unlucky householder who had his roof ruined that day.

This opens up quite a new possibility for understanding what Jesus said to the paralysed man. How would you feel if someone made a big hole in your roof? But Jesus looks down and says, with a rueful smile: "All right—I forgive you!" Something in his voice, though, made them all realize this was different.

5. Mark 2:5.

6. Luke 11:4.

7. N. T. Wright, *Matthew: 25 Studies for Individuals and Groups*, N. T. Wright for Everyone Bible Study Guides (Downers Grove, IL: InterVarsity, 2009), 39–40.

8. See Matt. 10:33.

9. John 20:21.

10. John 20:22–23.

11. Anthony De Mello, *The Way to Love: The Last Meditations of Anthony De Mello* (New York: Doubleday, 1992), 39.

12. 1 Cor. 5:5 NIV.

13. This quote is often attributed to Lewis B. Smedes from his book *The Art of Forgiving: When You Need to Forgive and Don't Know How* (New York: Ballantine Books, 1997).

14. 1 Cor. 5:5.

Chapter 13 Trials, Temptations, and Joys

1. James 4:14.

2. Heb. 2:15.

3. See Heb. 2:14–18.

4. Mark 9:49.

5. Matt. 27:46.

6. Acts 14:22.

7. Mark 4:17.

8. Bauer et al., *Greek-English Lexicon*, s.v. *peirasmos*.

9. James 1:2–4.

10. 1 Pet. 5:10, emphasis mine.

11. Eugene Peterson, *Run with the Horses* (Downers Grove, IL: Inter-Varsity, 2009), 74.

12. See Neh. 8.

13. Wright, *The Lord and His Prayer*, 48.

14. See 2 Cor. 1:3–6.

15. See Rom. 14.

16. See John 15:11.

17. See 1 Thess. 1:6–7.
18. Willard, *The Spirit of the Disciplines*, 79.
19. Peterson, *Run with the Horses*, 56.
20. See Matt. 16:17–19.
21. See Joel 2:1–11.
22. Joel 2:14.

Chapter 14 In the Name

1. V. 14.
2. V. 15.
3. Luke 11 is the only place where *anaideia* is found in Scripture.
4. Much of this section is inspired by the scholarship of Kenneth E. Bailey, former chair of the Biblical Department at the Near East School of Theology, Beirut.
5. Kenneth E. Bailey, *Poet and Peasant: A Literary Cultural Approach to the Parables* (Grand Rapids: Eerdmans, 1976).
6. John 10:30.
7. Heb. 1:3.
8. Andrew Murray Books, *Andrew Murray: With Christ in the School of Prayer*, Original Edition, Illustrated, Andrew Murray Books–Book 1, 2018, Kindle.
9. Matt. 16:15.
10. Matt. 16:16.
11. See 2 Pet. 1:4.
12. See 1 John 3:9.
13. John 20:17.
14. Matt. 18:20.
15. C. S. Lewis, *Til We Have Faces* (New York: HarperOne, 2017), 308.

Addison Bevere loves disassembling the boxes that fragment and frustrate our lives—a process he calls integrative faith. He is the author of *Saints* and coauthor of bestseller *The Holy Spirit: An Introduction*. Addison also serves as the COO of Messenger International, a discipleship organization that impacts millions of people in nearly every country. Father to four and husband to one, he spends most of his days in Tennessee. To connect with him visit AddisonBevere.com.

Free Courses, Audiobooks, and More to Help You Grow in Your Faith.

The MessengerX app is a revolutionary tool that connects you with world-class teachers, authors, and leaders who will help you embrace a vibrant faith in your everyday life.

Scan the QR code to download MessengerX

MessengerX

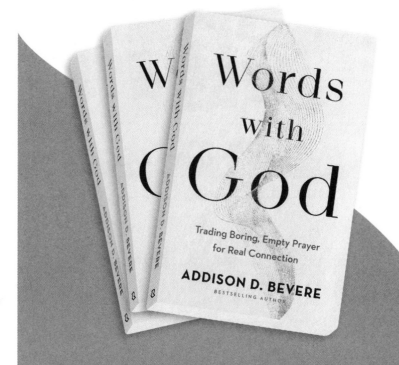

THE PODCAST ON DOING FAMILY WELL

at **home** with the Beveres

00:01   33:54

(15) ▶ (30)

1× ◉ •••

Tune in for intentional, lively, and meaningful conversations on how to navigate family well in this wonderful and crazy world.

Spotify   Listen on Apple Podcasts   ▶ YouTube   GET IT ON Google Play

A fresh look at faith for a world that's losing hope in religion.

Saints

BECOMING MORE THAN "CHRISTIANS"

ADDISON D. BEVERE

Foreword by MARK BATTERSON